MACROMEDIA®

50 Fast Flash™ MX Techniques

ELLEN FINKELSTEIN AND GURDY LEETE

MACROMEDIA®
50 FAST FLASH™ MX TECHNIQUES

Wiley Publishing, Inc.

50 Fast MACROMEDIA® **Flash™ MX Techniques**

Published by
Wiley Publishing, Inc.
10475 Crosspoint Blvd.
Indianapolis, IN 46256

`www.wiley.com`

Copyright © 2002 by Wiley Publishing, Inc., Indianapolis, Indiana

Manufactured in the United States of America

10 9 8 7 6 5 4 3 2 1

IV/RT/QZ/QS/IN

Published by Wiley Publishing, Inc., Indianapolis, Indiana
Published simultaneously in Canada

For general information on our other products and services or to obtain technical support, please contact our Customer Care Department within the U.S. at 800-762-2974, outside the U.S. at 317-572-3993 or fax 317-572-4002.

Wiley also publishes its books in a variety of electronic formats. Some content that appears in print may not be available in electronic books.

Library of Congress Cataloging-in-Publication Data

ISBN: 0-7645-3692-3

To MMY, who taught us a lot about techniques for the development of human life — they should be easy, enjoyable, and effective.

PREFACE

This book is named *50 Fast Flash MX Techniques*—it presents 50 relatively simple, yet exciting Flash MX techniques that you can do *quickly*. Some of these techniques may take 15 to 30 minutes, but many take far less time. They are also *easy* because all of the components are provided for you. You can copy them or add your own art.

This book is for anyone who wants to add some great techniques to a Web site in Flash but doesn't have the time to study Flash in-depth. Although many of the techniques involve considerable programming in ActionScript, Flash's programming language, you do not need to be a programmer to use the techniques. We have provided the ActionScript for you, and you can easily copy and paste it into your own movies.

WHY THIS BOOK WAS WRITTEN

When we were learning Flash, we quickly saw how powerful Flash is. We saw some amazing Web sites that used Flash. We also realized that some of the techniques were very involved. Like most people, we read the manual and looked up lots of questions in the online Help. We also read several books on Flash. All of these resources helped, but few provided us with the answer to our question, "How do you create the effect I saw on that Web site?"

When we wrote *Flash 5 For Dummies* and then updated it to *Flash MX For Dummies,* we felt we thoroughly covered the basics of Flash. Our feeling was confirmed by readers who told us that they started with no knowledge of Flash and were now creating Web sites. However, after a while, these readers were ready to move on—and the next steps were daunting — learning ActionScript and a deep, long study of Flash. They often wanted to know how to create specific techniques without having to get a master's degree in Flash.

There are numerous Flash Web sites that can help. They offer great tutorials and downloadable movies. Nevertheless, after a while, you can see so many sites that you can feel overwhelmed. When Wiley offered us the opportunity to write this book, we decided it was just what our readers needed.

THIS BOOK IS NOT LIKE MOST OTHER FLASH BOOKS

Although you can find many books on Flash, they typically have from 300 to 1,200 pages. Yet, the number of tutorials for getting a specific result is minimal. Books tell you how to use the program, but not how to put many aspects of the program together to get one result. When you turn to Flash, you usually want to achieve a certain result that you have either seen on another site or simply conjured up in your imagination — to make a line draw itself, turn a photograph into a drawn image, rotate a 3D logo, create a slide show with a blur effect, create mouse trails... The list can go on and on. Flash is an amazingly flexible program, and you could do so much with it, but how???

Our book offers the following:

- Fifty fast step-by-step techniques for your Web site
- Thirty-two full-color pages, most showing several stages of animation
- Over 50 royalty-free Flash movies (FLA files) on the CD-ROM, which contain the techniques, including the artwork and the ActionScript code
- All the Flash player movies (SWF files) on the CD-ROM, so you can quickly view each of the techniques in your browser, even without having Flash on your computer
- Tips and Notes to explain how to accomplish a task more easily or to provide additional information
- Special text formatting that allows you to quickly and easily complete a technique without reading the informative text
- Over 200 images portraying the techniques
- A CD-ROM that contains trial versions of Flash and Photoshop Elements
- A companion Web site at http://www.wiley.com/legacy/compbooks/Finkelstein, where you can click on a link for *50 Fast Flash MX Techniques.* Here you can find updates, a readers' gallery, and a list of online resources for more techniques. (See Appendix B for more information.)

WHO SHOULD READ THIS BOOK?

If you have never before used Flash, you should start with our *Flash MX For Dummies.* You need to understand the basic features of Flash and how to use them. From there, you can move straight on to this book.

This book is for anyone who knows the basics of Flash but is not an advanced user. If you have a Web site and want to use Flash to add features to your site, you'll find a huge amount of material here. Also, just by trying out the techniques as you follow the steps, you'll learn a great deal about Flash and what it can accomplish. Although each technique is very specific, all together they encompass most of Flash's capabilities.

Who knows? You may come up with your own techniques!

WHAT COMPUTER HARDWARE AND SOFTWARE WILL YOU NEED?

The minimum requirements to create a Flash movie are not high; you probably already have them on your computer. You'll be happier, however, with a faster computer, more memory (RAM), and a high-quality graphics card. You can use either a PC or a Mac — this book is an equal-opportunity knowledge provider.

Here are the minimum requirements provided by Macromedia for Windows:

- 200 MHz Intel Pentium processor
- Windows 98 SE, Windows Me, Windows NT4, Windows 2000, or Windows XP
- 64MB of free available system RAM (128MB recommended)

- 85MB of available disk space
- 1024 x 768, 16-bit (thousands of colors) color display or better
- CD-ROM drive

The requirements for the Macintosh are the following:

- Mac OS 9.1 and higher, or OS X 10.1 and higher
- 64MB of free available system RAM (128MB recommended)
- 1024 x 768, 16-bit (thousands of colors) color display or better
- CD-ROM drive

Luckily, Flash movies do not hog a lot of hard drive space. In fact, that's one of the advantages of Flash — movies load quickly on a Web site because they are small.

CONVENTIONS USED IN THIS BOOK

To make this book easy to use so that you can re-create the techniques quickly, we use a special format that focuses on the actual steps you need to take to complete the technique. Extraneous discussion is kept to a minimum.

The first page of each technique shows you the technique, often using four to eight frames, so you can visualize the animation. If the figure is shown in the color section, the figure number includes a color plate number (such as CP 1) in parentheses, so you can quickly find the image in color. Then we explain the technique in brief. We always refer you to the Flash movie on the CD-ROM so that you can immediately open it up and take a look.

We break up each technique into major steps and explain what each step accomplishes. Follow the bullet points to complete the technique on your own.

In each technique, we tell you to start with a new movie because sometimes working in an existing movie creates complications with existing ActionScript, movie clips, and so on. We suggest that you learn these techniques in a new movie first and then use your knowledge to add the techniques to existing movies.

CONTACT THE AUTHORS

We welcome comments from our readers. We do our best to answer all our e-mail, but note that we can't manage to provide technical support for all of Flash's many features. Contact Ellen Finkelstein at `ellenfinkl@bigfoot.com`. Contact Gurdy Leete at `gleete@mum.edu`.

ACKNOWLEDGMENTS

This book combines the knowledge, talents, and assistance of many people. We would like to thank the following people who contributed to this book.

Our major surprise contributor was Gurdy's wife, Mary Leete, who did all the programming for this book. With two kids (ages 5 and 7) playing around her, she managed to write some masterful code.

Tom Heine, Wiley Publishing, Inc.'s acquisition editor, offered us the opportunity to prepare a proposal for this book and supported us throughout the process of writing this book.

Amanda Peterson, the project editor, kept the book on track and handled innumerable details such as coordinating the editing and delivery to production. Amazing!

Kyle Bowen, the technical editor, refined our ActionScript so that it read correctly and made numerous helpful suggestions to make the explanations clearer.

Beth Taylor, the copy editor, made sure we were consistent with our spelling, capitalization, usage, and all those things that we could never have kept track of ourselves.

Mike Zak created the apple we use in Technique 40 and the cat in Technique 6.

Radim Schreiber (`www.radim.org`) took several beautiful photographs that we use for slide shows in Technique 23.

Dale Divoky (`ddivoky@mum.edu`) created the lovely artistic creations that we use for Techniques 36 and 42.

Joseph Rienstra (see `www.chira.com/j`) wrote the music for our MP3 player. You can find three of the pieces on his Web site as part of his online multiplayer game, Go-Krida, at `www.chira.com/j/g`.

We also want to thank our families for helping out and putting up with all the attention that went to this book (instead of to our families).

CONTENTS AT A GLANCE

PREFACE   VII

ACKNOWLEDGMENTS   XI

INTRODUCTION   XXIII

Chapter 1   2D Animation   1
Chapter 2   3D Animation   47
Chapter 3   Text   57
Chapter 4   Sound and Video   77
Chapter 5   Interactive Effects   85
Chapter 6   User Interfaces   113
Chapter 7   Mini Applications   175

APPENDIX A   WHAT´S ON THE CD-ROM   209

APPENDIX B   OTHER RESOURCES   213

ABOUT THE AUTHOR   215

COLOPHON   216

INDEX   217

END-USER LICENSE AGREEMENT   223

CONTENTS

PREFACE   VII

ACKNOWLEDGMENTS   XI

INTRODUCTION   XXIII

CHAPTER 1: 2D ANIMATION   1

TECHNIQUE 1
A LINE DRAWING ITSELF   3
For Complex Images   3
   Step 1: Draw the Image   3
   Step 2: Erase the Image   4
   Step 3: Reverse the Animation   4
For Simple, Linear Images   4
   Step 1: Draw the Image   4
   Step 2: Create the Coverup   4
   Step 3: Create the Shape Tween   5

TECHNIQUE 2
MAKE A CHARACTER WALK   7
   Step 1: Create Your Character   7
   Step 2: Create the First Position   8

Step 3: Create the Other Positions   9
Step 4: Move the Arms   9
Step 5: Levitate Your Character   9
Step 6: Fill in Your Character   9
Step 7: Create Forward Motion   9

TECHNIQUE 3
TALKING HEAD   11
   Step 1: Import the Sound File   11
   Step 2: Draw a Talking Head   12
   Step 3: Add the Mouth   13

TECHNIQUE 4
CREATE RIPPLES   15
   Step 1: Import a Photo   15
   Step 2: Create the Ripples   16
   Step 3: Shape Tween the Ripples   16
   Step 4: Add the Ripples to the Photo and Tween
     the Transparency   17

TECHNIQUE 5
DISOLVE A VECTOR
INTO A BITMAP   19
   Step 1: Import a Photo and Convert it
     to a Vector   19
   Step 2: Place the Photo on the Stage   20
   Step 3: Fade Out the Vector   20
   Step 4: Fade In the Bitmap Photo   20
   Step 5: Add a Stop Action at the End   20

TECHNIQUE 6
MORPH A GEOMETRIC SHAPE
INTO AN IMAGE   21
Morphing into a Photo   21
   Step 1: Import the Photo   21
   Step 2: Create an Outline   22

xv

Step 3: Fade Out the Outline   22
Step 4: Create a Shape Tween   22
Step 5: Fade in the Photo   23
Morphing into a Vector Image   24
Step 1: Draw the Shape   24
Step 2: Draw or Import the Graphic Image   24
Step 3: Create a Shape Tween   24

TECHNIQUE 7

MAKE BUBBLES   25

Step 1: Record Bubble and Popping Sounds   25
Step 2: Create the Bubble   26
Step 3: Make Bubble Variations   26
Step 4: Make a Bubble Wiggle   26
Step 5: Make a Tiny Bubble   27
Step 6: Create The Popping Animation   27
Step 7: Create Bubbles Bubbling Up and
    Popping   28
Step 8: Create the Final Bubble Movie   28

TECHNIQUE 8

KALEIDOSCOPE   31

Step 1: Create a Wedge   31
Step 2: Create the Kaleidoscope   32
Step 3: Create the Motion Tweens   32
Step 4: Create a Mask   33

TECHNIQUE 9

WARP AN IMAGE   35

Do the Wave   35
Step 1: Import an Image   36
Step 2: Create a Moving Bar Symbol   36
Step 3: Insert Instances and Make Each
    a Mask   36
Step 4: Add ActionScript   37
Step 5: Create a Mask   37

Do the Flip   38
Step 1: Import an Image   38
Step 2: Create a Motion Tween   38
Step 3: Complete the Revolution   38

TECHNIQUE 10

FIREWORKS   41

Step 1: Create the Beam   41
Step 2: Add ActionScript   42
Step 3: Position the Fireworks   45

CHAPTER 2: 3D ANIMATION   47

TECHNIQUE 11

ROTATING 3D LOGO   49

Step 1: Create the Logo   49
Step 2: Create the Rotation Effect   50
Step 3: Complete the Rotation   50

TECHNIQUE 12

ROTATING EARTH   53

Step 1: Import the Map   53
Step 2: Create the Earth   54
Step 3: Create the Motion Tween   54

CHAPTER 3: TEXT   57

TECHNIQUE 13
TEXT CONTROLLING OBJECTS   59
Step 1: Create a Symbol   59
Step 2: Add an Input Text Box   60
Step 3: Create a Button   60
Step 4: Add ActionScript to the Button   60
Step 5: Add Instructions   61

TECHNIQUE 14
ANIMATED TEXT WARPING   63
Flying Letters   63
Step 1: Create the Text   63
Step 2: Put Each Letter on a Separate Layer   64
Step 3: Create a Set of Smaller Letters   64
Step 4: Move the Smaller Text to Frames   64
Step 5: Create the Shape Tween   64
Step 6: Stagger the Letters   65
Step 7: Add a Keyframe at the End   65
Growing Letters   65
Step 1: Create the Text   65
Step 2: Distribute the Letters to Layers   65
Step 3: Squish the Letters   66
Step 4: Distribute the Squished Letters
    to Layers   66

Step 5: Create the Shape Tweens   66
Step 6: Stagger the Tweens   66

TECHNIQUE 15
TEXT MORPHING   67
Step 1: Create the Text   67
Step 2: Break Apart the Text   67
Step 3: Create the Image   67
Step 4: Create the Shape Tween   68

TECHNIQUE 16
MOVIES INSIDE TEXT   69
Step 1: Create or Open the Animation   69
Step 2: Add the Text and Make it a Mask   70

TECHNIQUE 17
SWARMING DOTS FORM TEXT   71
Step 1: Create the Text   71
Step 2: Make the Dots   72
Step 3: Move the Dots   72
Step 4: Place the Dots on the Text   73

TECHNIQUE 18
RADIATING TEXT EFFECTS   75
Step 1: Create the Text   75
Step 2: Soften the Edges   75
Step 3: Create a Shape Tween   76
Step 4: Make the Text Glow   76

CHAPTER 4: SOUND AND VIDEO   77

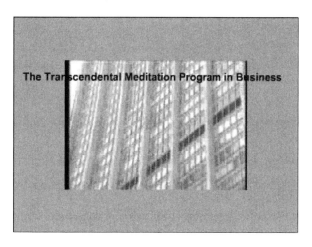

TECHNIQUE 19

ON/OFF AND VOLUME SOUND CONTROLS   79

Step 1: Create a Button   79
Step 2: Create the Slider Bar   80
Step 3: Assemble the Buttons and Slider Bar   80
Step 4: Import the Sound   80
Step 5: Add the ActionScript   81

TECHNIQUE 20

ADDING VIDEO TO A FLASH MOVIE   83

Step 1: Import the Video File   83
Step 2: Specify the Video Settings   84

CHAPTER 5: INTERACTIVE EFFECTS   85

TECHNIQUE 21

DRAGGABLE MAGNIFYING LENS   87

Step 1: Draw the Magnifying Glass   87
Step 2: Import an Image to Magnify   88
Step 3: Create the Magnified Image   88
Step 4: Make the Magnifying Glass Draggable   88
Step 5: Bring in the Scene and Add ActionScript   88

TECHNIQUE 22

DRAGGABLE MOVIES   91

Step 1: Prepare Your Movie as a Symbol   91
Step 2: Resize the Movie Clip   92
Step 3: Make a Button   92
Step 4: Make a Movie Clip   92
Step 5: Insert the Draggable Movie   93

TECHNIQUE 23

IMAGE SLIDE SCROLLER WITH MOTION BLUR   95

Step 1: Create the Filmstrip   95
Step 2: Create the Buttons   96
Step 3: Insert the Large Images   96
Step 4: Add the Motion Blur   97

TECHNIQUE 24

PAN AND ZOON AN IMAGE   99

   Step 1: Import an Image   99
   Step 2: Make a Button   100
   Step 3: Create a Mask   100
   Step 4: Add the ActionScript for the Frames   100
   Step 5: Add the ActionScript for the Buttons   102

TECHNIQUE 25

MAKE A SCROLLING VIRTUAL REALITY PANORAMA   103

   Step 1: Import a Panoramic Image   103
   Step 2: Place and Tween the Image   104
   Step 3: Convert the Animation to
     a Movie Clip   104
   Step 4: Create a Mask   105

TECHNIQUE 26

DRAGGABLE MASK   107

   Step 1: Create the Background   107
   Step 2: Create a Movie Clip   107
   Step 3: Create a Button   108
   Step 4: Make the Movie Clip Draggable   108
   Step 5: Set Up the Mask   108

TECHNIQUE 27

INTERACTIVE SHADOWS   109

   Step 1: Create the Text   109
   Step 2: Create the Cursor   110
   Step 3: Add The ActionScript   110
   Step 4: Place the Symbols on the Stage   110

CHAPTER 6: USER INTERFACES   113

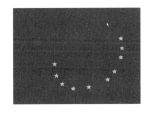 

TECHNIQUE 28

MOUSE TRAILS   115

   Step 1: Create the Trailing Graphic   115
   Step 2: Create a Background   116
   Step 3: Add ActionScript   116

TECHNIQUE 29

TABBED MENU   119

   Step 1: Create the Layers   119
   Step 2: Create the Bar   120
   Step 3: Create the Tabs   120
   Step 4: Create the Chosen Tab   120
   Step 5: Extend the Other Layers   121
   Step 6: Add Labels   121
   Step 7: Add Content   121

TECHNIQUE 30

SCROLL BARS   123

   Step 1: Insert a ComboBox   123
   Step 2: Create a Scrolling Dynamic Text Box   124
   Step 3: Add the Background   125
   Step 4: Add the ActionScript   125

TECHNIQUE 31

POP-UP WINDOWS   127

    Step 1: Create the Pop-Up Window   127
    Step 2: Set Up the Pop-Up Window   128
    Step 3: Add a Button to Display the
       Pop-Up Window   128

TECHNIQUE 32

CREATE A MULTIPLE CHOICE

QUIZ   131

    Step 1: Create the Layers   131
    Step 2: Add Radio Buttons for
       Answer Choices   131
    Step 3: Add the Question   132
    Step 4: Add the "Next" Button   132
    Step 5: Add a Scoring Screen   132
    Step 6: Add the ActionScript   133

TECHNIQUE 33

USER RESPONSE FORM   135

    Step 1: Create Text Boxes   135
    Step 2: Add a Button   136
    Step 3: Create the Second Frame   136
    Step 4: Create the Third Frame   136
    Step 5: Add the ActionScript   136

TECHNIQUE 34

FORM VALIDATION   139

    Step 1: Create the Text Boxes   139
    Step 2: Insert a Pushbutton   140
    Step 3: Create the Next Screen   140

    Step 4: Add the ActionScript   140
    Step 5: Add a Background   142

TECHNIQUE 35

COLLAPSIBLE MENU   143

    Step 1: Create Buttons For Menu Items   143
    Step 2: Add Actions For the Menu Frames   144
    Step 3: Add Actions For the Menu Movie
       Clips   144
    Step 4: Create the Submenus   146
    Step 5: Place the Menus on the Timeline   146

TECHNIQUE 36

3D BOOK AS A USER INTERFACE   149

    Step 1: Create the Left Page   149
    Step 2: Create Images For the Book   151
    Step 3: Create Animation For the Pages   151
    Step 4: Add Other Left Pages Turning   151
    Step 5: Add Stop Actions   152
    Step 6: Return to the First Page   152

TECHNIQUE 37

ROLLOVER SCROLL   153

    Step 1: Create the Arrow Buttons   153
    Step 2: Create a Filmstrip   154
    Step 3: Make a Mask and Background   154
    Step 4: Add ActionScript   154

TECHNIQUE 38

CUSTOM CURSORS   157

    Step 1: Create the Graphic or Animation   157
    Step 2: Add ActionScript   158

TECHNIQUE 39
CASCADING MENU 159

Step 1: Create a Button 159
Step 2: Create the Menu 160
Step 3: Add Actionscript to the Buttons 160
Step 4: Compile the Menu 161
Step 5: Add ActionScript For the Menu 162

TECHNIQUE 40
ANIMATED BUTTON 165

Step 1: Create the Image For the Button 165
Step 2: Create the Animation 166
Step 3: Create the Button 166
Step 4: Place the Button on the Stage 166

TECHNIQUE 41
PRELOADER WITH PROGRESS DISPLAY 167

Step 1: Create the Preloader Box 167
Step 2: Create the Preloader Animation 168
Step 3: Add ActionScript 168
Step 4: Create the Scenes and Main Movie 169

TECHNIQUE 42
SLIDE SHOW WITH SPECIAL EFFECT TRANSITIONS 171

Step 1: Set Up the Slides 171
Step 2: Create a "Next" Button 172
Step 3: Insert the Slides 172
Step 4: Add Some Actions 172
Step 5: Create the Effects Layer 172
Step 6: Create the Transition Effects 173

CHAPTER 7: MINI-APPLICATIONS 175

TECHNIQUE 43
NEWS TICKER 177

Step 1: Create the Text 177
Step 2: Add ActionScript 178
Step 3: Create the Text Box 179

TECHNIQUE 44
DIGITAL OR ANALOG CLOCK 181

Digital clock 181
Step 1: Create a Symbol with ActionScript 181
Step 2: Create the Clock 182
Analog Clock 182
Step 1: Create the Hands 183
Step 2: Add the Date/Text Box 183
Step 3: Add ActionScript 183
Step 4: Draw the Clock 184

TECHNIQUE 45

MUSIC KEYBOARD AND

SYNTHESIZER 185

    Step 1: Create the Piano Keyboard 185

    Step 2: Import the Sounds 186

    Step 3: Add ActionScript 186

TECHNIQUE 46

MP3 PLAYER 189

    Step 1: Create the Artwork 189

    Step 2: Add the Buttons 190

    Step 3: Add the Counter 191

    Step 4: Add the ActionScript 191

TECHNIQUE 47

DRUM SET 195

    Step 1: Create the Drumhead 195

    Step 2: Create the Snare Drum 196

    Step 3: Place the Drums on the Stage 196

    Step 4: Draw the Bass Drum and Cymbal 196

    Step 5: Import the Sounds 197

    Step 6: Add ActionScript 197

TECHNIQUE 48

ON-SCREEN PAINT PROGRAM 199

    Step 1: Make the Buttons 199

    Step 2: Add ActionScript 200

TECHNIQUE 49

CALCULATOR 203

    Step 1: Create the Artwork 203

    Step 2: Add the Text Box 204

    Step 3: Add ActionScript 204

TECHNIQUE 50

CREATE A STAND-ALONE MOVIE 207

    Step 1: Publish the Movie 207

    Step 2: Play the Movie 208

APPENDIX A 209

WHAT'S ON THE CD-ROM 209

APPENDIX B 213

OTHER RESOURCES 213

ABOUT THE AUTHORS 215

COLOPHON 216

INDEX 217

INTRODUCTION

You may be tempted to skip this Introduction and go directly to the techniques, but you will find some very helpful advice and techniques here that will help you use the techniques more smoothly and with fewer hassles.

WHAT IS FLASH AND WHEN SHOULD YOU USE IT?

Macromedia Flash is animation software that is most often used for Web sites. (It can also be used on CD-ROMs and even TV.) Flash is a full-featured program and can create almost any technique you can imagine. On the other hand, you may not want to use Flash all the time. Although Flash's vector images are compact and files are compressed when published, Flash still introduces an overhead to your Web site. Make sure that you don't make your viewers wait too long for your site to load. In general, a good guideline is that you should use Flash only when it doesn't violate two basic principles of good Web site design:

- Fast loading
- Easy to use (usability)

WHAT YOU NEED TO KNOW BEFORE BEGINNING THE TECHNIQUES

This book is not a "How to Use Flash" book and assumes that you know the basics. As we mentioned in the Preface, if you need to learn the basics, read our *Flash MX For Dummies*, which contains all the knowledge you need for using these techniques.

Flash is not a program that you can just open and use. At the very least, you should be familiar with the following features of Flash before trying these techniques:

- Starting a new movie, saving, and publishing
- Using the Toolbox
- Selecting and editing objects
- Using the Library
- Using panels, including the Property inspector and the Actions panel
- Using the Timeline, including working with frames and keyframes
- Using Layers, including locking and hiding layers

- Creating and editing symbols (movie clips, graphic symbols, and buttons)
- Specifying the Stage size and color
- Working with vector and bitmap images
- Creating tweens and frame-by-frame animation
- Importing and using sounds

HELPFUL HINTS

You will find yourself using several features of Flash over and over. Here we list some helpful hints to make using Flash more efficient.

1. FLASH MOVIES INVOLVE BOTH ART AND SCIENCE

Flash movies should look good and that's the artistry. The science involves the ActionScript programming and how you use Flash's features. As you use these techniques, feel free to create your own artwork or use ours. You'll soon figure out how to meld the two.

2. USE MULTIPLE LIBRARIES AT ONCE

If you have our Flash movie open as well as your own, you can copy artwork and ActionScript from one movie to the other. The artwork is in the Library. With two movies open, choose Window ➢ Library. You will see the libraries of both movies, as shown in the following. (If necessary, open the Library again in the second movie.) Here are some useful techniques when working with multiple libraries:

- Click the collapse/expand arrow to collapse or expand the Library for any individual movie.
- Double-click the title bar to collapse the entire Library when you need to see the entire Stage.
- If the libraries are not combined, drag the dragger of one Library onto the other Library until they join.

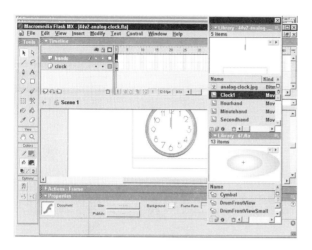

3. COPY AND PASTE ACTIONSCRIPT

You don't want to type all the ActionScript code from scratch. Instead, you can copy and paste it. We always explain exactly where to find it in our sample movie on the CD-ROM. Follow these steps:

Open the movie containing the ActionScript.

Select the frame, button, or movie clip that contains the ActionScript.

Open (Window ➤ Actions) or expand the Actions panel.

Click the View Options button, shown here, and choose Expert Mode.

Drag down the left side of all the ActionScript (making sure to include the very last line) to select it.

Press Ctrl+C (Win) / ⌘+C (Mac) to copy the code to the Clipboard.

Open your movie. If it's already open, choose it from the bottom of the Window menu.

Select the frame, button, or movie clip where you want the ActionScript to go.

Open or expand the Actions panel.

Click in the ActionScript text area.

Press Ctrl+V (Win) / ⌘+V (Mac) to paste the code into the Actions panel.

If you have trouble finding the ActionScript — you can't find it by selecting the appropriate symbol or frame — open the Movie Explorer (Window ➤ Movie Explorer). Be sure the Show ActionScripts button is active. Look for the listing of the symbol or frame indicated in the text. To select the ActionScript, click the first line, then press Shift and select the last line. Then copy and paste the ActionScript as described in the previous steps.

4. CENTER OBJECTS ON THE STAGE

We often tell you to center an object on the Stage. You can center an object in two ways:

- If you haven't scrolled vertically or horizontally and the Stage is still in the center of your display, select the object, and cut it by pressing Ctrl+x (Win) / ⌘+x (Mac). Then immediately paste it by pressing Ctrl+v (Win) / ⌘+v (Mac).
- If you have scrolled either vertically or horizontally, you need to use the longer technique. Choose Window ➤ Align to open the Align panel. Click the To Stage button and then click both the Align Vertical Center and Align Horizontal Center buttons.

5. RETURN TO THE MAIN TIMELINE

When you create a symbol, you are "inside" the symbol — in symbol-editing mode. When you're done, you need to return to the main Timeline. The easiest way is to click Scene 1 or the back arrow just below the layer listing, as shown in the following figure.

6. EXPAND AND COLLAPSE THE PROPERTY INSPECTOR AND ACTIONS PANEL

You use the Property inspector and Actions panel a lot in Flash, but you don't want them open all the time — they take too much room on your screen. In fact, the Actions panel covers the entire Stage. One useful configuration is to keep the Property inspector and Actions panel open, but collapsed at the bottom of the screen, as shown below. To expand either panel, click its arrow on the panel's title bar.

The Property inspector has an expanded size that contains additional controls. Here you see the Property inspector in its smaller size. Click its expand/collapse arrow to open it up further.

7. SELECT FRAMES ON THE TIMELINE

When selecting a range of frames before tweening the frames, you can use one of two techniques:

- Click the first keyframe, press Shift, and click the last keyframe. This technique includes all the frames and the two keyframes in the tween. If you add another keyframe in a later frame, a new tween to the new keyframe is created.
- Click once between the two keyframes. This technique results in the same animation, but the last keyframe is not tweened. If you add another keyframe in a later frame, no new tween is created.

We generally use the first instruction because it seems cleaner, but the second method is a little faster and may be just what you want.

8. TEST YOUR MOVIES

Simple animation can be played by pressing Enter. All other movies need to be *tested*. Press Ctrl+Enter (Win) / ⌘+Return (Mac). Flash publishes the movie using the current settings and creates the SWF file. A new window opens where you will see the animation. Click the window's close button to return to the Flash authoring environment.

9. SAVE VERSIONS

When working with complex Flash movies, it helps to save several versions as you try out experimental techniques. Especially when you take one of the techniques in this book and insert it into an existing movie, it's safest to make a copy of the existing movie and try it out on the copy. A simple method is to add "v1", "v2", and so on at the end of your movie file names.

OVERVIEW OF THE TECHNIQUES

The 50 techniques in this book are grouped into seven chapters. You can do them in any order or just look at the ones that interest you. The later chapters, especially Chapters 5, 6, and 7 make use of 2D animation, of course, but if you understand animation (motion and shape tweening as well as frame-by-frame animation), you don't need to do the 2D animation techniques first.

How do you decide which techniques you want to look at? First read the description of the technique and look at the figures. Then open the SWF file on the CD-ROM and see if you like it.

Chapter 1 covers 2D animation techniques. Of course, animation is the very basis of Flash, and you won't want to miss these. Each technique manipulates an image in a different way. Some of the techniques could apply to any type of image, such as the warping techniques. Others are more specific, like our kaleidoscope and fireworks. You'll certainly find something you like.

Chapter 2 offers two simulated 3D animation techniques — a rotating logo and a rotating earth. Unfortunately, Flash is a solidly 2D program, but you can make your viewers swear that you're animating in 3D. After all, a screen is flat, so even true 3D animation is translated into 2D.

Chapter 3 provides several text-related techniques, including breaking text apart and combining objects to create words. If you want to animate text, you've come to the right place.

Chapter 4 covers sound and video. The first is a set of buttons that turns sound on and off and changes the volume. This technique is almost a must if you have a Web site with music or any loud sounds. The second technique explains how to incorporate video into your movies — a new feature for Flash MX.

Interactive effects are an important feature of Flash, and we cover them in Chapter 5. These include several types of draggable buttons, a pan/zoom tool, and a 360° panorama. You'll be able to incorporate these techniques into many situations.

Flash is capable of creating an entire Web site, including the user interface. Flash MX introduces *components,* just for the purpose of adding scroll bars, check boxes, and so on. Chapter 6 offers a number of user-interface techniques, such as several menus, a quiz, a mouse trail, an animated button, and a preloader.

Chapter 7 goes the full distance to develop a few mini-applications. We have a calculator, an MP3 player, a simple paint program, a cool drum set, a clock, and a news ticker. Some are seriously useful, but most are just for fun. So enjoy!

CHAPTER 1

2D ANIMATION

Flash is basically a 2D animation program. In this chapter, you'll discover some basic techniques that you can use in a myriad of ways to create exciting animation.

Technique 1 shows you how to create an image drawing itself, as if an invisible pencil were drawing the image in front of your eyes. Because the viewer doesn't know what the end result will look like, using this technique is a fun way to create anticipation and surprise. In Technique 2, you learn how to animate a simple figure. Technique 3, another cartooning effect, creates a talking head. Here you create several mouth positions and sync them with the sound of the words.

In Technique 4, you learn how to produce a ripple effect, like the ripples on a pond — very soothing! In Technique 5, you discover how to dissolve a vector graphic into a bitmap, in this case, a photo. Technique 6 shows how to morph a geometric shape into an image, such as a cat or a face. Technique 7 creates bubbles rising in water.

Technique 8, the kaleidoscope, is a cool 1960s effect. Technique 9 warps any image, distorting it in some way, to create a cool effect. Technique 10 displays fireworks shooting into the sky.

A LINE DRAWING ITSELF

1.1 (CP 1)

FOR COMPLEX IMAGES

This movie is a great example of using animation to make a static drawing come alive. The drawing implies movement, but the animation makes the drawing process explicit. Many Flash animations use a simple procedure of successively uncovering a line or portion of an image (more about that later), but that technique is awkward when you are working with a complex drawing. The technique that we explain here works with all types of drawings, although it results in a larger file size.

In a nutshell, you create a drawing and use frame-by-frame animation to erase a little bit of the drawing in each keyframe. Then you reverse the animation.

STEP 1: DRAW THE IMAGE

In a new movie (choose **File ➢ New**), use the Flash drawing tools to create any image. You can also import an image and use **Modify ➢ Break**

Apart or **Modify** ➢ **Trace Bitmap**. We imported an image that had been modified in Adobe Photoshop.

STEP 2: ERASE THE IMAGE

Decide the order in which you want your image to appear. Plan out the path that the imaginary pencil will take. Start from the section of the image that will appear last in the animation. (Remember, you will reverse the frames.)

- Choose the **Eraser** tool. In the **Options** section of the **Toolbox**, choose a shape (square probably works best) and a size (depends on your image). Erase the section that will appear last, as shown in **Figure 1.2**. Press **F6** in Frame 2 to create a keyframe and then press **Esc** to deselect the image.
- Repeat the process, continuing to erase small sections of the image in the reverse order it will appear, until the entire image has been erased.

STEP 3: REVERSE THE ANIMATION

Save your movie and then select all the keyframes you have created. (Click the first keyframe, press **Shift**, and click the last keyframe.) Choose **Modify** ➢ **Frames** ➢ **Reverse**. Choose **Control** ➢ **Play** to play the animation.

FOR SIMPLE, LINEAR IMAGES

For simpler, more linear images, you can use another technique that creates a very small file size. Cover up the image with a shape that matches the background of your movie and then shape tween it from full size to very small. As the cover-up shape gets smaller, the image is progressively revealed.

STEP 1: DRAW THE IMAGE

In a new movie, use Flash's drawing tools to create any image.

> **TIP**
>
> If your background is solid, you can use the Paintbrush tool instead of the Eraser tool. Choose a fill color that matches the movie background and progressively cover up the image instead of erasing it.

STEP 2: CREATE THE COVERUP

- Choose **Insert** ➢ **Layer** to add a new layer. Rename it *coverup*.
- Choose the **Rectangle** tool. Change the **Fill Color** to match the background of your movie. Change the **Stroke Color** to **No Color**. Draw a shape that covers up the entire image. If necessary, use the **Free Transform** tool to modify the rectangle's shape or rotation so that the image is completely covered.

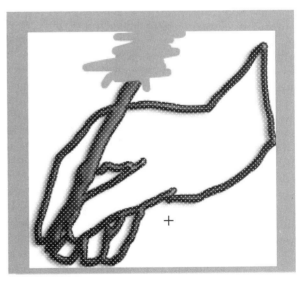

1.2

STEP 3: CREATE THE SHAPE TWEEN

Now you want to shape tween the cover-up shape so that it covers everything in the beginning of the animation and covers nothing at the end.

■ Click a frame that you want to be the last keyframe of the animation. Press **F6** to create the keyframe.

> **NOTE**
>
> To see this movie, open **01a.fla** from the Techniques folder of the CD-ROM. Choose Control ➢ Test Movie to see the animation.

> **NOTE**
>
> Look for **01b.fla** in the Techniques folder of the CD-ROM for an example of this technique.

■ Change the shape of the cover-up so that it no longer covers the image. For example, make a wide rectangle very narrow. You can use the **Free Transform** tool to reshape the cover-up shape.

■ Select all the keyframes you have created. (Click the first keyframe, press **Shift**, and click the last keyframe.)

■ If necessary, display the **Property inspector**. (Choose **Window** ➢ **Properties**.) In the **Property inspector**, choose **Shape** from the **Tween** drop-down list. Choose **Control** ➢ **Play** to play the animation, as shown in **Figure 1.3**.

1.3

2

MAKE A CHARACTER WALK

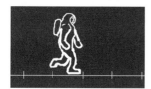

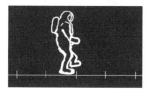

2.1 (CP 2)

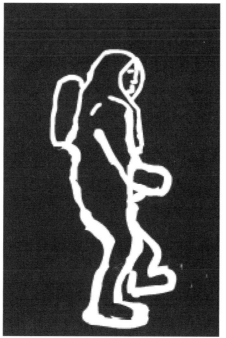

2.2

Flash has spawned an entire Flash-cartooning industry. Cartooning can be time-consuming and difficult, but it's also lots of fun. This simple technique shows you how to make a character walk.

Cartooning is usually frame-by-frame animation. The movements are too complex for tweening. By keeping the keyframes close together, you can create the appearance of smooth animation.

STEP 1: CREATE YOUR CHARACTER

Start with a new movie (**File ➢ New**). You need a line drawing of a character in profile. It should be fairly simple, like the astronaut shown in **Figure 2.2**. A slight roughness of the stroke is helpful to hide imperfections as you make adjustments to the arms and legs.

NOTE

Look for the walking astronaut in **02.fla** in the Techniques folder of the CD-ROM.

You can draw the character by using the Flash tools, or you can import a JPEG (as long as it isn't copyrighted) by choosing **File ➤ Import**. Then choose **Modify ➤ Trace Bitmap**.

STEP 2: CREATE THE FIRST POSITION

First, concentrate on the legs, which are obviously the most involved in walking. The walking process utilizes eight positions:

1. The left leg stiffens as it prepares to hit the ground.
2. The left leg bends as it gets ready to push off.
3. The left leg lifts up the body as the right foot lifts and swings forward.
4. The right foot is at its high point.
5. The right leg stiffens as it prepares to hit the ground.
6. The right leg bends as it gets ready to push off.
7. The right leg lifts up the body as the left foot lifts and swings forward.
8. The left leg is at its high point.

Of course, unless your character is not going very far, this sequence is repeated over and over. One sequence equals two steps.

You need to decide how long it takes for your character to complete the cycle. If it should take about a second, and your movie is set to the default 12 frames per second, then the cycle must be completed in about 12 frames on the Timeline. However, for smooth walking, you probably want to create keyframes either every frame or every other frame.

Depending on your artwork, you may have to modify the original character to match one of the eight positions. You can do this using any of the Flash tools. Here's one way to change the position of the legs.

■ Choose the **Pencil** tool and a stroke color that contrasts with the color of the strokes in your character. (The **Ink** modifier of the **Pencil** tool is useful because it changes your lines very little.) Use the **Pencil** tool to draw a line where one of the legs (that you want to move) meets the hips, as shown in **Figure 2.3**. The entire leg is now segmented from the rest of the character — amputated, you could say.

■ Move the leg away from the rest of your character's body and make changes. To change its angle, use the **Free Transform** tool to rotate the leg.

2.3

■ When you're done, move the leg back into place, and your character is whole again.

STEP 3: CREATE THE OTHER POSITIONS

To create the next position, add a keyframe (**F6**) where you want the next position. Then follow the same procedure described in Step 3 to create the next position. Continue this procedure until you're done.

STEP 4: MOVE THE ARMS

The arms swing opposite the legs. As the left leg moves forward, the right arm moves forward. Go back and segment each arm individually and rotate it to the desired position and then move it back. Each arm goes back and forth once in a walking cycle.

STEP 5: LEVITATE YOUR CHARACTER

At stages three and seven in the cycle, the body lifts up a little. Raise the character slightly at these points to create a bouncing stride. For a statelier walk, lengthen the leg on the ground slightly and move the entire character up a little. A horizontal line on a separate layer is helpful here. Lock the layer so that the line doesn't move.

STEP 6: FILL IN YOUR CHARACTER

You may want to fill in the strokes with some colorful clothing at this point. Use the Paint Bucket tool.

STEP 7: CREATE FORWARD MOTION

Your character wants to go somewhere. You can create forward motion in two ways. The most obvious is to move your character in the direction of the walk at each keyframe. However, after awhile, your character will be off the Stage, and no one will be able to see it.

Another method is to create a background and animate the background to move in the opposite direction of the walking character.

Test your movie (**Control** ➢ **Test Movie**) to see your character walk.

TIP

You can use onion-skinning to see all the frames at once. You can then make minor adjustments for smoother animation. Click the Onion Skin button below the Timeline to turn on onion-skinning.

3

TALKING HEAD

3.1

Here's another cartooning technique — a talking head. Of course, you can attach it to a body if you want. This technique involves synchronizing mouth shapes to the words. It's lots of fun.

STEP 1: IMPORT THE SOUND FILE

Start with a new movie (**File ➢ New**). You'll either import an existing sound file or record your own. If you record your own, you can use Sound Recorder in Windows or SimpleSound on the Mac. In either case, you end up with a sound file.

■ Choose **File ➢ Import**, locate the sound file, and click **Import**. You can import AIFF, WAV, and MP3 sounds. The sound file is now in the Library.

11

■ Rename **Layer 1** to *sound*. Click **Frame 1** (or the keyframe where you want the sound to go). Open the Library (**Window ➢ Library**) and drag the sound over the Stage.

■ In the **Property inspector** (**Window ➢ Properties**), choose **Stream** from the **Sync** drop-down list. (You may need to click the **Expand/collapse** arrow at the lower-right corner of the Property inspector to see the **Sync** drop-down list.)

■ Add a keyframe (**F6**) where you want the sound to end. The Property inspector lists the sound's statistics including the number of seconds, so you can calculate the ending keyframe by multiplying the seconds by the number of frames per second in your movie (shown at the bottom of the Timeline).

STEP 2: DRAW A TALKING HEAD

It's time to draw your head.

■ Add a new layer. Call it *head*.

■ Draw your head using the Flash tools or import a photo (**File ➢ Import**) and choose **Modify ➢ Trace Bitmap** to convert it to a vector drawing.

NOTE

You'll find two movies in the Techniques folder of the CD-ROM that relate to this technique: **03a.fla** and **03b.fla**. The first is the final movie of the talking head. The second is just a set of mouth positions that you can copy and use in your talking heads. It also functions as a guideline for creating mouths and is shown in **Figure 3.2**.

EDITING SOUNDS IN FLASH MX

You should edit a sound if it contains any silent areas to reduce its size. Also, you may want to adjust the volume or add special effects.

To edit a sound, click a frame that contains a sound. Choose Window ➢ Properties to open the Property inspector if it is not already open. Click the Edit button to open the Edit Envelope dialog box, in the following figure.

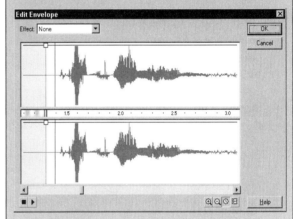

Between the left (top) and right (bottom) channel display is a narrow strip that controls the starting and ending points of a sound. Along this strip is a vertical bar at the beginning and the end of the sound. The Time In control is at the left edge of the sound and specifies the start of the sound. Drag it to the right to delete the beginning of the sound. The Time Out control is at the right edge of the sound and specifies the end of the sound. Drag it to the left to delete the end of the sound.

In both the left and right channel displays, Flash shows an envelope line to indicate the approximate direction of the sound's volume. There are small squares (*envelope handles*) where the volume changes. Drag an envelope handle up (to increase volume) or down (to decrease volume).

When you finish editing a sound, click OK to close the Edit Envelope dialog box.

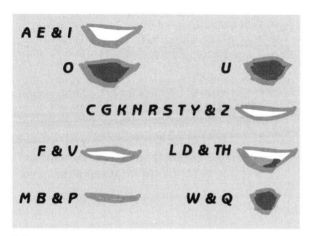

3.2

STEP 3: ADD THE MOUTH

Now add the mouth shapes.

- Add a layer above the *face* layer and call it *lips*.
- Drag the **Playhead** from left to right, listening to the sound. You can do this because you set your sound to stream. Using the chart (**Figure 3.2**), decide in which frames you need to change the shape of the mouth and add a keyframe (**F6**) in each of those frames.
- Now you need to draw the mouths. Because you often need the same shape more than once, we suggest that you draw all the mouths on the first keyframe you are using and then place

them to the side of the Stage. Label them with the sound to which they go, or you can number them according to their order. In this way, you can also make sure that all the mouths are of similar sizes. (You don't want the mouth to suddenly grow or shrink, just change shape.)

- For each keyframe, **copy** the mouth you need, click the keyframe, and **paste** in the mouth. Drag it to the proper location.
- When you're done, make any necessary adjustments to the face around the mouth. You may need to change other parts of the expression, such as the eyes.
- Drag the **Playhead** across the timeline again and make sure that the mouth doesn't seem to jump in any direction at a keyframe. If it does, use the arrow keys to move it slightly.

Test the movie and watch your head talk!

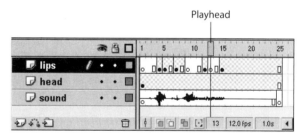

3.3

CREATE RIPPLES

4.1 (CP 3)

T hrow a stone in a pond, and you see concentric ripples. This effect is beautiful and easy to create.

STEP 1: IMPORT A PHOTO

Start with a new movie (**File** ➢ **New**). A photo of water is an obvious choice. Still water works best because your ripples don't have to compete with the waves in the photo.

15

- Choose **File** ➢ **Import** and choose your photo.
- With the photo selected, press **F8** to turn it into a symbol. Name it *photo*. Delete it from the **Stage**.
- Add a layer and call it *photo*. With the **photo** layer active, open the **Library** (**Window** ➢ **Library**) and drag an instance of the *photo* symbol onto the Stage.
- With the symbol still selected, open the **Property inspector** (**Window** ➢ **Properties**) and choose **Alpha** from the **Color** drop-down list. Set the alpha to 85%.
- Add a keyframe (press **F6**) at Frame 45.

STEP 2: CREATE THE RIPPLES

The ripples are just concentric ovals, alternating in black and white. We used ovals because of the angle of the photo. If your photo looks straight down on a pond (a bird's eye view), you should use true circles.

- Choose **Insert** ➢ **New Symbol** to start a new symbol.
- Create a black-filled oval with no stroke about the size of the largest ripple you want (which depends on your photo). Copy and paste it; then drag the copy off the original circle. Change the fill to white. Choose **Modify** ➢ **Transform** ➢ **Scale** and Rotate (**Ctrl+Alt+S on Windows**/⌘+**Option+S on a Mac**). Scale the oval to **90%** and move it back over of the original oval, centering it.
- Continue the same process, copying and pasting, dragging off the previous oval, scaling down, changing the color (alternately to black and

white), and dragging the oval back on the previous ones, until you have as many ovals as you want. The symbol should look something like the one in **Figure 4.2**.
- Select all the circles and center them around the registration point of the symbol (the small plus sign).

STEP 3: SHAPE TWEEN THE RIPPLES

Concentric ripples expand, so you want the ripples to start small and end up how you created them.

- Insert a keyframe at about Frame 45 (press **F6**).
- Click Frame 1. Click the **Free Transform** tool and drag from any corner to make the ripples small. Recenter them around the symbol's registration point.
- Select all the frames. In the **Property inspector** (**Window** ➢ **Properties**), select **Shape** from the **Tween** drop-down list.
- Click Scene 1 to return to the main Timeline.

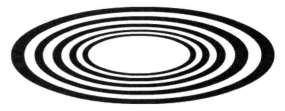

4.2

STEP 4: ADD THE RIPPLES TO THE PHOTO AND TWEEN THE TRANSPARENCY

You're now ready to add the ripples to the photo. Because ripples disappear as they get bigger, you also add a tween that makes them gradually become transparent.

- Rename Layer 1 to *ripples*.
- With the *ripples* layer selected, drag the *ripples* symbol from the Library onto the photo where you want to see the ripples.
- Add a keyframe (**F6**) at Frame 45. Select all the frames and choose **Motion** from the **Tween** drop-down list of the **Property inspector.**
- Click Frame 45 and then click the ripples. In the **Color** drop-down list of the **Property inspector**, choose **Alpha** and set the alpha to 0.

If you're having trouble seeing the ripples because of the photo, click the **Eye** column of the *photo* layer to hide it. Your photo may also need a lower alpha level than the 85 percent we previously recommended, depending on the qualities of the photo.

Test the movie to watch the ripples ripple outward!

> **NOTE**
>
> You can find the ripples in the Techniques folder of the CD-ROM in **04.fla.**

DISSOLVE A VECTOR INTO A BITMAP

5.1 (CP 4)

I n this technique, you import a photo, trace it to a bitmap, and then dissolve it back to its photo form, as if a painting is turning into a photo. It's very easy to do.

STEP 1: IMPORT A PHOTO AND CONVERT IT TO A VECTOR

In this step, you import a photo and trace it to a vector drawing. Then you turn it into a symbol and center it on the Stage.

- Start with a new movie (**File ➤ New**). Import a photo (**File ➤ Import**). Immediately choose **Modify ➤ Trace Bitmap**. We used the following settings:

  - **Color threshold:** 90
  - **Minimum area:** 16 pixels

19

- **Curve Fit:** Normal
- **Corner Threshold:** Normal

- Scale the image, if necessary, to take up most of the **Stage**. Choose **Modify ➢ Scale and Rotate** and remember by what percent you scaled the image.
- Convert the image to a symbol (**Insert ➢ Convert to Symbol**) and name it *vector*. Cut and paste it to center it on the **Stage**.
- Rename the layer to *vector*. Lock and hide the layer.

NOTE

Photo from U. S. Fish and Wildlife Service (`http://gimp-savvy.com/PHOTO-ARCHIVE/`)

STEP 2: PLACE THE PHOTO ON THE STAGE

You make a symbol of the photo and center it on the Stage on a separate layer.

- Add a new layer called *bitmap*.
- From the **Library** (**Window ➢ Library**), drag the photo onto the **Stage**.
- Scale the image the same percent you used for the vector image.
- Convert the photo to a symbol (**Insert ➢ Convert to Symbol**) named *bitmap*. Cut and paste it to center it on the **Stage**.
- Lock and hide the *bitmap* layer.

STEP 3: FADE OUT THE VECTOR

Now you create a motion tween that fades from 100% alpha to 0% alpha.

- Select the *vector* layer. Unlock and unhide it.
- Add a keyframe at Frame 30. Select all the frames from 1 to 30. In the **Property inspector** (**Window ➢ Properties**), choose **Motion** from the **Tween** drop-down list.

- Click Frame 1. Click the instance. In the **Property inspector**, choose **Alpha** from the **Color** drop-down list. Make sure that it is set to 100%.
- Click Frame 30. Click the instance. In the **Property inspector**, choose **Alpha** from the **Color** drop-down list. Set the alpha to 0%.
- Lock and hide the layer.

STEP 4: FADE IN THE BITMAP PHOTO

Now you create a motion tween that fades in the photo.

- Select the *bitmap* layer. **Unlock** and **unhide** it.
- Add a keyframe at Frame 30. Select all the frames from 1 to 30. In the **Property inspector** (**Window ➢ Properties**), choose **Motion** from the **Tween** drop-down list.
- Click Frame 1. Click the instance. In the **Property inspector**, choose **Alpha** from the **Color** drop-down list. Set it to 0%.
- Click Frame 30. Click the instance. In the **Property inspector**, choose **Alpha** from the **Color** drop-down list. Set the alpha to 100%.

STEP 5: ADD A STOP ACTION AT THE END

Add a stop action at the last frame so that the movie doesn't loop, which ruins the fade-in effect by jumping the movie from the last frame back to the beginning.

- Add a new layer and name it *actions*.
- Click Frame 30 of the *actions* layer and add a keyframe (**F6**).
- In the **Actions** panel (**Window ➢ Actions**), choose **Actions ➢ Movie Control**. Double-click the **stop** action.

Play the movie to see the effect.

NOTE

You can find this technique in **05.fla**, which is in the Techniques folder of the CD-ROM.

6

MORPH A GEOMETRIC SHAPE
INTO AN IMAGE

6.1 (CP 5)

T his technique is impressive but easy to do. A shape morphs into a photo. You start with a shape, such as a circle. The circle changes to an outline of your photo. Then the outline fades out as the photo fades in. Later in this section, we use an example of a circle morphing into a cat to explain the process of simple shape tweening, which you can use for line drawings.

MORPHING INTO A PHOTO

In this technique, you morph a circle into a photo. You can find an example of this technique in the Techniques folder of the CD-ROM. Look for 06a.fla.

STEP 1: IMPORT THE PHOTO

Start with a new movie (**File ➢ New**). Then import the photo and prepare it by removing its background and converting it to a symbol.

- Import the photo (**File** ➢ **Import**).
- Change the name of Layer 1 to *photo*.
- Choose **Modify** ➢ **Break Apart**. You may have to do this more than once. (You know that you're done when the **Break Apart** item is no longer available on the **Modify** menu.)
- Use the **Eraser** tool to erase the background and leave just the head, as shown in **Figure 6.2**. (You can use the entire figure in a photo if you want.)
- Choose **Insert** ➢ **Convert to Symbol**. Name it *head* and click OK. Delete the symbol from the **Stage**.

STEP 2: CREATE AN OUTLINE

Now, create an outline around the photo.

- Drag an instance of the *head* symbol onto the **Stage** from the **Library**. (If the **Library** isn't open, choose **Window** ➢ **Library**.)
- Add a layer. Call it *outline*.
- Working at a 200% or 400% zoom, use the **Paintbrush** tool to draw an outline around the head, as shown in **Figure 6.3**. (If you have a tablet with a pen, you'll find doing this part easier than if you're trying to draw with a mouse.) The color should be the same as the shape you want to morph from. For example, if you want to morph from a gray circle, use a gray fill for the outline.
- Choose **Insert** ➢ **Convert to Symbol** and name it *outline*. Click **OK**.

STEP 3: FADE OUT THE OUTLINE

- Add keyframes (**F6**) at Frames 10 and 20. Click Frame 1 and delete the outline symbol. It now exists between Frames 10 and 20.
- Click Frame 20 and then click the outline symbol. If necessary, open the **Property inspector** (**Window** ➢ **Properties**). From the **Color** drop-down list, choose **Alpha** and set the alpha to 0).
- Create a motion tween between Frames 10 and 20. Select all the frames between 10 and 20 and choose **Motion** from the **Tween** drop-down list on the **Property inspector**. You now have a tween that fades out the outline symbol.

STEP 4: CREATE A SHAPE TWEEN

Now you're ready to create a shape tween from a circle (or another shape you choose) to the outline shape. An oval may be a nice choice because many people have oval-shaped faces, and the resulting shape tween is subtler.

6.2

6.3

■ Double-click the *outline* symbol in the **Library** to edit it. Select the outline on the Stage and copy it to the **Clipboard**. Choose **Edit ➢ Document** to return to the main **Timeline**. Create a new layer and name it *shape*. Paste in the outline and line it up with the one on the *outline* layer.

■ Add keyframes at Frame 12 and 13. Click in Frame 13 and delete the outline.

■ Click Frame 1. Delete the outline and replace it with a circle by using the same color and width as the outline. Then select the circle and choose **Modify ➢ Shape ➢ Convert Lines to Fills**. Because the outline is a fill, you'll get a better shape tween if the circle is also a fill.

■ Select Frames 1 through 12 and choose **Shape** from the **Tween** drop-down list in the **Property inspector.**

STEP 5: FADE IN THE PHOTO

The last part is to fade in the photo.

■ Select the *photo* layer. Add keyframes at Frames 10 and 20. Delete the photo from Frame 1.

■ Click Frame 10 and then click the head symbol. In the **Property inspector**, choose **Alpha** from the **Color** drop-down menu and set it to 0.

■ Select Frames 10 through 20 and choose **Motion** from the **Tween** drop-down list in the **Property inspector**. You now have a tween that fades in the photo.

Test the movie. You should see your circle tween to the outline and then to your photo.

> **NOTE**
>
> See **06b.fla** in the Techniques folder of the CD-ROM for our example of morphing a circle into a cat.

6.4

MORPHING INTO A VECTOR IMAGE

In this technique, you morph a circle into a cat, as shown in **Figure 6.4**. Now that you aren't using a photo, your task is much easier. Flash can shape tween any shape into any other shape. You can use any bitmap that you import and break it apart or trace it. For best results, make sure that both your graphic image and your shape are made up of strokes or of fills but not both. Otherwise, you'll end up with gray shapes in the middle of the tween. Also, the shapes should not be a symbol or grouped.

STEP 1: DRAW THE SHAPE

Draw a shape using the Flash tools. Add a keyframe where you want the animation to end and delete the shape you drew.

STEP 2: DRAW OR IMPORT THE GRAPHIC IMAGE

Click the last keyframe. Draw or import a graphic. If you import a graphic, break it apart and use the **Eyedropper tool** to turn everything to strokes (if you're working with strokes). You can also use the **Trace Bitmap** feature.

STEP 3: CREATE A SHAPE TWEEN

Select all the frames of the tween and choose **Shape** from the **Tween** drop-down list of the **Property inspector**.

Play the movie to see the tween effect.

> **NOTE**
>
> If you want to work with fills, select the shape and choose Modify ➤ Shape ➤ Convert Lines to Fills.

MAKE BUBBLES

7.1 (CP 6)

B ubble, bubble, fun, no trouble. These bubbles aren't hard to make; however, you can be as ambitious as you want. Part of the fun was making the bubbling and popping sounds, which we made using our tongue and lips.

STEP 1: RECORD BUBBLE AND POPPING SOUNDS

Of course, you don't need to add sounds, but if you want them, you can record your own sounds by using Sound Record (Windows) or

NOTE

Photo from the National Oceanic and Atmospheric Administration/Department of Commerce (www.photolib.noaa.gov/reef/index.html)

Simplesound (Mac). Save the files as bubbles.wav (or bubbles.aif) and pop.wav (or pop.aif).

STEP 2: CREATE THE BUBBLE

Create your bubble. You'll reuse this bubble in variations for all the bubbles. Of course, you can make bubbles however you want, but here are instructions for ours. (You can also copy the bubbles in **07.fla** on the CD-ROM.)

- Draw a circle with no stroke. Press **Shift** to make it a perfect circle.
- Open the **Color Mixer** (**Window** ➢ **Color Mixer**) and choose **Radial** from the **Fill Style** drop-down list.
- Click the left marker. Click the **Fill Color** button and choose a color for the center of the bubble. We used a light green (#99FFCC in hexadecimal).
- Click the right marker. Click the **Fill Color** button and choose a color for the outside of the bubble. We used a light purple (#9999FF in hexadecimal).
- The **Fill Color** button on the toolbox now displays your radial fill. Click the **Paint Bucket** tool and then click the selected circle to fill it with the new radial fill.

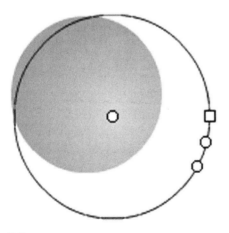

- Click the **Fill Transform** tool on the toolbox and then click the circle. You should see a ring around the circle, as shown in **Figure 7.2**.
- Drag the center point down and to the right, as you see in **Figure 7.2**. You may also want to make the radial fill smaller, which you do by dragging the middle circular handle on the ring inward.
- Choose the **Paintbrush** tool and pick a white fill. Choose a small brush from the **Options** section of the toolbox. At the upper-left side of the bubble, draw a slightly curved line and a dot to represent highlights.
- Choose **Insert** ➢ **Convert to Symbol**. Choose the **Graphic** behavior, name it *big-bubble,* and click OK.

STEP 3: MAKE BUBBLE VARIATIONS

Now you make smaller bubbles, one opaque and one semi-transparent.

- With *big-bubble* still selected, choose **Modify** ➢ **Transform** ➢ **Scale and Rotate**. Scale the bubble to 25% and click **OK. Choose Insert** ➢ **Convert to Symbol**. Choose the **Graphic** behavior, name it *opaque-bubble,* and click **OK**.
- With *opaque-bubble* still selected, choose **Alpha** from the **Color** drop-down list of the **Property inspector** (**Window** ➢ **Properties**). Set the alpha to 50%. Choose **Insert** ➢ **Convert to Symbol**. Choose the **Graphic** behavior, name it *bubble,* and click **OK**.
- Delete the bubble on the Stage.

STEP 4: MAKE A BUBBLE WIGGLE

You want the bubbles to wiggle a little as they rise.

- Choose **Insert** ➢ **New Symbol**. Make it a movie clip named *bubble-movie* and click **OK**.

7.2

- Add a layer and call it *sound*. Click the first frame and drag the *bubbles* sound onto the **Stage**. Add a keyframe at Frame 15.
- Drag an instance of *bubble* onto the center of the Stage.
- Add a keyframe (**F6**) at Frame 5. Move *bubble* up and to the right about 20 pixels — not far. Select **Frames 1 through 5** and choose **Motion** from the **Tween** drop-down list of the Property inspector (**Window** ➤ **Properties**).
- Add a keyframe at Frame 10. Move *bubble* in the direction of its original location but a little farther.
- Add a keyframe at Frame 15. Move *bubble* to its second location (at Frame 5) again.
- Click **Scene 1** to return to the main Timeline.

STEP 5: MAKE A TINY BUBBLE

When a bubble pops, it creates tiny bubbles.

- Choose **Insert** ➤ **New Symbol**. Make a graphic symbol called *tiny-bubble*.
- Drag *bubble* from the **Library** onto the center of the **Stage**.
- Zoom in to **200% or 400%**. Choose the **Free Transform** tool. Hold **Shift** while you drag in a corner handle and make the bubble very small. Check the bubble at **100%** to make sure that it isn't too small to see.
- Choose **Scene 1** to return to the main Timeline.

STEP 6: CREATE THE POPPING ANIMATION

Now you want to create the animation of bubbles popping. You add the *pop* sound here.

- Choose **Insert** ➤ **New Symbol**. Make a movie clip symbol called *pop*.

> **NOTE**
>
> You can find our bubbles in the Techniques folder of the CD-ROM in **07.fla**.

- Rename **Layer 1** to *pop*. Import your *pop* sound.
- Add a keyframe at Frame 5. Drag the *pop* sound onto the **Stage.**
- Add a keyframe at Frame 12.
- Add five new layers. Name one *bubble*. Name the others *tiny bubble1, tiny bubble2, tiny bubble3,* and *tiny bubble4.*
- Drag an instance of *bubble* to the center of the **Stage.**
- On each of the *tiny bubble* layers drag an instance of *tiny bubble* to the center of *bubble.*
- Add a keyframe at Frame 12 for each of the other layers.
- For each of the *tiny bubble* layers, click the keyframe on Frame 12, move the selected *tiny bubble* instance a little away from the *bubble* in four different directions, select **Frames 1 through 12**, and choose **Motion** from the **Tween** drop-down list of the **Property inspector** (**Window** ➤ **Properties**). Your **Stage** should look like **Figure 7.3.**
- Click the keyframe on Frame 12 of the *bubble* layer. Click the *bubble* instance. From the **Color** drop-down list of the **Property inspector**, choose **Alpha** and set the alpha to 0 because the main bubble disappears when it bursts.
- Add a keyframe at Frame 16 of each of the *tiny bubble* layers. For each layer, click Frame 16, click the selected *tiny bubble*, choose **Alpha** from the **Color** drop-down list of the **Property inspector**,

and set the alpha to 0%. (The **Property inspector** defaults to its last setting, so all you have to do is choose **Alpha** and the setting will be at 0%.) Doing this makes the tiny bubbles disappear also.

■ Click **Scene 1** to return to the main **Timeline**.

STEP 7: CREATE BUBBLES BUBBLING UP AND POPPING

In this step, you combine *bubble-movie*, which wiggles bubbles, and *pop*, which pops them, to create an animation that lets the bubbles rise.

■ Choose **Insert** ➤ **New Symbol** and create a movie clip named *bubbles*.

■ Add seven new layers for a total of eight. Name them *bubbles1*, *pop1*, *bubbles2*, *pop2*, *bubbles3*, *pop3*, *bubbles4*, and *pop4*.

■ With Frame 1 of the *bubbles1* layer selected, drag *bubble-movie* somewhere in the lower-left quadrant of the **Stage**. Add a keyframe at Frame 12. Move the instance of *bubble-movie* up to the middle of the screen and a little to the right. Select Frames 1 through 12 and choose **Motion** from the **Tween** drop-down list of the **Property inspector**. Lock the *bubbles1* layer.

■ Add a keyframe at Frame 12 of the *pop1* layer. Drag an instance of the *pop* movie clip on top of *bubble-movie*. Add a keyframe at Frame 40 of the *pop1* layer.

■ Do these last two points for each of the four sets of bubbles/pop layers but start each set five frames to the right. So the *bubbles2* tween goes from Frame 5 to Frame 17. (Of course, you can make adjustments as you want. This technique just times the bubbles so that they rise one after another.) Put each instance of *bubble-movie* in a different location, along the lower part of the

Stage, and move each one up at a slightly different angle.

■ Click **Scene 1** to return to the main **Timeline**.

STEP 8: CREATE THE FINAL BUBBLE MOVIE

After creating all those graphic and movie clip symbols, you're finally ready to put them together in one, big, bubbly movie.

■ Import a background image. Choose **Insert** ➤ **Convert to Symbol** to convert it to a graphic symbol, called *background*. Rename Layer 1 *background*. Add a keyframe at Frame 50.

■ Add a new layer, *big-bubble*. Drag the *big-bubble* graphic symbol onto the bottom-center of the **Stage**, even half below the **Stage**. Create a keyframe at Frame 50. In Frame 50, move *big-bubble* a little above the **Stage**. Select Frames 1 through 50 and choose **Motion** from the **Tween** drop-down list of the **Property inspector**. If you want to fade out this bubble, click Frame 50, click *big-bubble*, and then choose **Alpha** from the **Color** drop-down list of the **Property inspector**. Choose 25% (or 0% to fade it out completely).

■ Create a new layer, *some bubbles*. Add a keyframe at Frame 15. Drag an instance of *bubbles* to a location at the bottom of the **Stage**.

> **TIP**
>
> You can choose File ➤ Open as Library and open **09.fla**. Click the first frame of your *pop* layer and drag *pop.wav* from the **09.fla** Library.

■ Create a new layer, *more bubbles.* Add a keyframe at Frame 10. Drag an instance of *bubbles* to a different location at the bottom of the **Stage**.

■ Add another layer, *even more bubbles.* Add a keyframe at Frame 5. Again drag an instance of *bubbles* to a different location at the bottom of the **Stage**.

■ Insert a new layer, *mask.* Drag it to the top of the layer list, if necessary. Draw a filled rectangle the size of the **Stage**. Right-click (Win)/Ctrl-click (Mac) and choose **Mask** from the menu. The layer below *mask* is indented on the list. To include all the other layers in the mask, drag each of the other layers inward and slightly upward to indent it.

Test your movie. You may want to move the location of each instance of *bubbles.* Enjoy your bubbles!

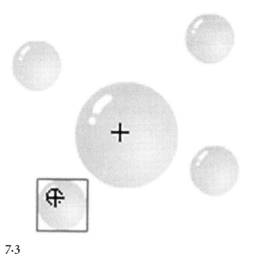

7.3

KALEIDOSCOPE

8.1 (CP 7)

Do you remember looking into a kaleidoscope when you were a kid — turning the tube and being amazed? You can create a similar effect in Flash. You can create infinite variations by choosing different tweens.

STEP 1: CREATE A WEDGE

Start with a new movie (**File ➢ New**).

You may remember that a kaleidoscope is divided into wedge-shaped sections. Creating the wedge is easy.

1. Draw a circle that covers most of the visible **Stage** when the zoom is at 100%. You need only the stroke on the circumference. You can delete any fill. Press the **Shift** key as you use the **Oval** tool to create a perfect circle.

2. Select the circle. Cut and paste it to center it onto the **Stage**. (This works only if you haven't scrolled to move the view of the Stage; otherwise, use the **Align** panel.)

3. On the side of the circle, use the **Line** tool to draw a vertical line that is a little longer than the diameter of the circle. Press the **Shift** key as you draw to make it perfectly vertical.

4. Copy the line to the **Clipboard** and paste it. The line will be centered on the **Stage** and across the circle.

5. With the line still selected, choose **Modify ➤ Transform ➤ Scale and Rotate**. In the **Rotate** text box, enter **22.5** and press **Enter**.

6. Select the line still remaining on the side of the circle. Cut and paste it to center it, as shown in **Figure 8.2**.

7. Delete everything except the wedge shape as shown in the figure. All the lines are segmented so that you can easily delete the segments you don't need.

8. Select the wedge and choose **Insert ➤ Convert to Symbol**. Name it *wedge,* keep the movie clip default, and click **OK**.

9. Delete the *wedge* symbol on the **Stage**. (You have it saved in the **Library**.)

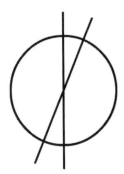

8.2

STEP 2: CREATE THE KALEIDOSCOPE

Now you want to create a circle of wedges, creating the look of a kaleidoscope.

1. Rename **Layer 1** to *wedges*.

2. Open the **Library** (**Window ➤ Library**) and drag in an instance of the *wedge* symbol. Place the instance at the top-center of the **Stage**, in approximately the same position it occupied originally when you created it.

3. With the wedge still selected, choose the **Free Transform** tool. Drag the transformation point — the circle at the center of the wedge — to the lower-left corner of the wedge.

4. Copy the wedge to the **Clipboard**. Choose **Edit ➤ Paste in Place** (**Ctrl+Shift+V** (Win)/ ⌘**+Shift+V**(Mac)).

5. Choose **Modify ➤ Transform ➤ Scale and Rotate** (**Alt+Ctrl+S** (Win)/**Option+**⌘**+S**(Mac)). In the **Rotate** text box, enter **22.5** and press **Enter**.

6. Repeat Steps 4 and 5 until the circle is completely filled up with wedges. (Using the keyboard shortcuts makes this process go faster.)

7. Click the *wedges* layer to select everything on the layer. Choose **Insert ➤ Convert to Symbol**. Name the symbol *kaleidoscope,* keep the default movie clip behavior, and click **OK**.

STEP 3: CREATE THE MOTION TWEENS

You now have a lot of wedges. To create the kaleidoscope effect, you now create a symbol of shapes to tween in the *wedge* symbol. When you're done, each of the wedges becomes animated.

■ Double-click *wedge* in the **Library** (**Window ➤ Library**) to edit it.

- Rename the existing layer to *wedge*. Insert a new layer and drag it below the existing layer. Call it *shapes*. Lock the *wedge* layer.
- On the *shapes* layer, create several shapes in bright colors. You'll get the best results with bright colors. Thick contrasting strokes also create a nice effect. We used circles and ovals. You want to fill up most of the wedge and extend out to the left with lots of shapes. **Figure 8.3** shows the symbol that we created.
- Click the *shapes* layer to select all the shapes. Choose **Insert ➤ Convert to Symbol** and call the symbol *shapes*.
- Click the symbol and look at its X and Y coordinates in the **Property inspector** (**Window ➤ Properties**). Write them down. You want the shapes to end up in the same position at the end of their motion tween journey so they don't jump when the movie loops.
- On the *shapes* layer, add a keyframe at Frame 20. Click Frame 20 and move the shape symbol to the right, but make sure that it still covers the wedge. Select Frames 1 through 20 and choose **Motion** from the **Tween** drop-down list of the **Property inspector**.
- Add a keyframe at Frame 40. Move the *shapes* symbol back to its original coordinates (you can type them in the **X** and **Y** text boxes of the **Property inspector**). Select Frames 20 through 40 and choose **Motion** from the **Tween** drop-down list of the **Property inspector**. This time select **CW** (clockwise) from the **Rotate** drop-down list and set the tween to rotate 1 time in the **Times** text box.

STEP 4: CREATE A MASK

Now you want to turn the wedge into a mask, hiding everything outside of the wedge shape. All you see is the shape tweens, repeated inside every wedge shape.

- Unlock the *wedge* layer.
- Use the **Paint Bucket** tool to fill in the *wedge* symbol.
- **Right-click** (Win)/**Ctrl-click** (Mac) the *wedge* layer and choose **Mask** from the menu. The wedge disappears.

Test your movie and prepare to be hypnotized!

8.3

WARP AN IMAGE

9.1

This technique takes a photo or any image and warps it to create a groovy effect. The "groovy" is literal, because the effect works by creating narrow panels, or grooves. Although setting up this effect takes some time, after you do, you can change the ActionScript to create different effects with the same grooves. We show you two variations on this theme — one variation creates a wavy effect, and the other creates a flipping effect, as if the image is on a sheet of paper, and you're flipping it around a vertical axis.

DO THE WAVE

This version looks as if a wave is flowing through the image. Or perhaps as if the image is being alternately squished and expanded.

STEP 1: IMPORT AN IMAGE

First you import an image, turn it into a symbol, and resize it to fill up the Stage.

■ Start with a new movie (**File ➢ New**). Choose **File ➢ Import** to import a photo or any image.
■ Choose **Insert ➢ Convert to Symbol** and name it *photo*. Click **OK**.
■ Use the **Free Transform** tool to make sure that the photo covers the entire **Stage.** In these instructions, we assume that the **Stage** is the default 400 pixels high.
■ Add a keyframe at Frame 21 (**F6**) to bring the photo out to Frame 21.

STEP 2: CREATE A MOVING BAR SYMBOL

Now you create a rectangle, motion tween it from the top of the photo to the bottom, and turn it all into a symbol.

■ Add a new layer. Keep the default name, **Layer 2**.
■ Choose the **Rectangle** tool and set the stroke to **No Stroke**. Draw a rectangle the same width as the image and 20 pixels high.
■ Choose **Insert ➢ Convert to Symbol** and call it *line*. Click **OK**.
■ Move the bar over the top part of the photo. Choose **View ➢ Snap to Objects** or zoom in to position the bar precisely.
■ Add a keyframe in Frame 21 of **Layer 2**. Move the bar to the bottom of the image, again positioning it precisely. Select all the frames and choose **Motion** from the **Tween** drop-down list on the **Property inspector**. The bar should move from the top of the photo to the bottom.

■ To turn everything on the **Stage** into a symbol, select both layers. (Click the first layer name, press **Ctrl** (Win)/⌘ (Mac), and then click the second layer name.) Choose **Edit ➢ Copy Frames**. Press **Esc** or click outside the **Stage** to make sure that no objects are selected and choose **Insert ➢ New Symbol**. Make it a movie clip and call it *mask 1* and click **OK**. Click the first frame and choose **Edit ➢ Paste Frames**.
■ Click **Scene 1** below the layer listing to return to the main Timeline.

STEP 3: INSERT INSTANCES AND MAKE EACH A MASK

Now you delete what's on the main Timeline and insert the *mask 1* symbol on 20 separate layers. Then you turn each symbol instance into a mask.

■ Select the frames on Layer 1. **Right-click** (Win)/ **Ctrl-click** (Mac) and choose **Remove frames**. Add a keyframe (**F6**) in Frame 1. Then do the same for Layer 2.
■ Click the **Add Layer** button on the **Timeline** 19 times so that you have a total of 21 layers.
■ Click the first frame of Layer 21. Open up the **Library** (**Window ➢ Library**) and drag an instance of the *mask 1* symbol onto the Stage. In the **Property inspector** change the **X** text box value to 0. Do the same for the **Y** text box value, to position the symbol instance exactly. Then type *m21* in the **Instance Name** text box, which is also in the **Property inspector**.

TIP

After you have drawn the rectangle, open the Property inspector (Window ➢ Properties). With the rectangle selected, you can see the height (marked H) in the lower-left corner. Type 20 and press Enter to change the height of the rectangle to 20 pixels. You can set the width to match the width of the photo in this way, too. Select the photo and check its width in the Property inspector. Then select the bar and type the same number in the W (width) text box of the Property inspector.

- Create a keyframe (**F6**) in Frame 2 of Layer 20. Drag an instance of *mask 1* onto the Stage. As you did for Layer 21, position the instance at X=0, Y=0. Give it an instance name of *m20*.
- Continue to repeat this process for each of the layers down to Layer 1, starting each layer in the next frame, placing it at X=0, Y=0, and giving it an instance name that matches the number of the layer.

(This sounds like it takes a long time, but you can probably do it in less than five minutes.)

- Click **Layer 1** and then double-click the instance on the Stage to edit it. **Right-click** (Win)/ **Ctrl-click** (Mac) Layer 2 (the top layer that contains the *line* symbol) and choose **Mask** from the menu.
- Select Frame 23 in all the layers and add a frame (**F5**).

STEP 4: ADD ACTIONSCRIPT

Now you add ActionScript to set the xscale of each mask in a wavy pattern, which mirrors the effect from top to bottom.

- In the main movie Timelines, add a new layer and call it *actions*.

TIP

Use the Align panel (Window ➢ Align) to line up each instance.

- On the *actions* layer, add keyframes at Frames 21, 22, and 23.
- Click Frame 21. Open the Action panel (**Window ➢ Actions**). Click **View Control** and choose **Expert** mode. Add the following ActionScript. You can paste it in from Frame 21 of the *actions* layer of **09a.fla**, which is on the CD-ROM.

```
for (i=1;i<=12;i++){
j=88+(i*2);
setProperty("m"+i,_xscale,j);
}
for (i=12;i<=21;i++){
j=110-((i-12)*2);
setProperty("m"+i,_xscale,j);
}
```

- Click Frame 23. In the **Action** panel, type the following or paste it in from Frame 23 of the *actions* layer of **09a.fla**.

```
gotoAndPlay(22);
```

- For each layer, create a keyframe in Frame 23.

STEP 5: CREATE A MASK

To hide the edges of the effect, create a mask around the edges.

TIP

You can change "xscale" in both places in the ActionScript to "yscale" to create a different wave effect.

NOTE

You can find the yscale version in the Techniques folder of the CD-ROM as **09b.fla**.

- Add a new layer. Call it *mask*. It must be on top of all the other layers.
- Zoom so you can see the entire Stage. A zoom of 50% usually works.
- Draw a filled rectangle the size fo the **Stage**. **Right-click** (Win)/**Ctrl-click** (Mac) and choose **mask** from the menu. The layer below *border* is indented on the list. To include all the other layers in the mask, drag each of the other layers inward and slightly upward to indent it.

Test the movie to see the effect!

DO THE FLIP

This technique is very, very easy, and you can easily apply it to any image or photo. Basically, you just turn the image into a symbol and create a motion tween that flips the symbol, as shown in **Figure 9.2**. It looks like a 3D effect.

STEP 1: IMPORT AN IMAGE

Start with a new movie (**File** ➤ **New**). Import an image and turn it into a symbol.

- Import an image or photo (**File** ➤ **Import**).
- Select the image and choose **Insert** ➤ **Convert to Symbol**. Name it *myPicture*.

STEP 2: CREATE A MOTION TWEEN

Create the motion tween that flips the symbol.

- Add a keyframe (**F6**) at Frame 21.
- Choose **Modify** ➤ **Transform** ➤ **Scale.** Drag the middle-left handle all the way to the right, flipping your symbol, as shown in **Figure 9.3**.
- Select all the frames from 1 through 21 and choose **Motion** from the **Tween** drop-down list of the **Property inspector** (**Window** ➤ **Properties**).

Play the movie to see the effect; it looks as if the symbol is a sheet of paper being turned around.

STEP 3: COMPLETE THE REVOLUTION

The first motion tween only turns the sheet around 180 degrees. Now you complete the cycle to 360 degrees.

- Select the symbol. Choose **Insert** ➤ **Convert to Symbol**. Name it *myPicture2*.
- Add a keyframe at Frame 22. In the **Tween** drop-down list of the **Property inspector**, choose **None** to remove the motion tween. Delete the current symbol.

9.2

NOTE

You'll find this technique in **09c.fla** in the Techniques folder of the CD-ROM.

■ From the Library (**Window** ➢ **Library**), drag in *myPicture2* onto Frame 22 and center it on the Stage.

■ Add a keyframe at Frame 42.

■ Choose **Modify** ➢ **Transform** ➢ **Scale**. As you did earlier, drag the middle-left handle to almost the center of the **Stage** so that your symbol is very narrow. Then drag the middle-right handle all the way to the left, flipping your symbol.

■ Select all the frames from 22 through 42 and choose **Motion** from the **Tween** drop-down list of the Property inspector (**Window** ➢ **Properties**). Test the movie to see the result.

USING THE MOVIE EXPLORER TO TROUBLESHOOT

The Movie Explorer is a great way to troubleshoot movies. In a movie as complex as this one, you can open the Movie Explorer (Window ➢ Movie Explorer), click the Show Frames and Layers button, and check that each layer has the right instance, for example. You can also click the Show Action Scripts button and view the ActionScript. Click any plus (+) sign (Win) or right pointing triangle (Mac) to expand the display. In the Find text box, you can enter any expression to search the entire movie. For example, you can search "goto" to find that expression in your ActionScript.

TIP

You can choose the Free Transform tool from the toolbox instead of the menu.

9.3

FIREWORKS

10.1

Fireworks denote fun and excitement. They're a great way to introduce a new product or service. These fireworks flicker and move. Even better, the ActionScript finds random sizes, colors, and path lengths for the fireworks, so you never know exactly how they'll show up!

The fireworks are a combination of animation and ActionScript programming. This technique involves a lot of steps, but none are difficult. You can copy and paste the ActionScript code from the movie on the CD-ROM, so don't worry about that part.

STEP 1: CREATE THE BEAM

This animation creates one "beam" of each firework.

- Start with a new movie (**File ➢ New**).
- Choose **Insert ➢ New Symbol**, give it the **movie clip** behavior, name it *myBeam,* and click **OK**.

NOTE

Look for the fireworks in **10.fla** in the Techniques folder of the CD-ROM.

10.2

■ Change the zoom factor to 800. Create a small black circle (about 7 pixels across) with no stroke (just fill) on the registration point. Use the **Horizontal scrollbar** to scroll the registration point to the left side of your screen.

■ Select the circle and choose **Insert ➤ Convert to Symbol**. Name it *Dot*.

■ Insert a keyframe (**F6**) in Frame 4. Click Frame 4 and move *Dot* about 6 pixels to the right. Select Frames 1 through 4 and choose **Motion** from the **Tween** drop-down list of the **Property inspector** (**Window ➤ Properties**).

■ Insert a keyframe in Frame 5. Delete *Dot*. In its place, draw a rectangle with a fill only, about 16 pixels wide and 2 pixels high. Choose **Insert ➤ Convert to Symbol** and name it *Ray*.

■ Insert a keyframe in Frame 12. Click Frame 12 and move *Ray* almost to the right side of the screen (at 800% zoom). Use the **Free Transform** tool to make the rectangle narrower, about 9 pixels. Select Frames 5 through 12 and click **Motion** from the **Tween** drop-down list of the **Property inspector**.

■ Insert keyframes in Frames 13 and 14 and in each frame move *Ray* slightly to the right and make it a little narrower from side to side. You should now be at about the middle of your screen.

■ Insert a keyframe at Frame 15. Delete the rectangle and in its place draw a "sparkle" as shown in **Figure 10.2**. We did this by drawing two rectangles, choosing **Modify ➤ Transform ➤ Scale and**

Rotate, and rotating one by 45 degrees and the other by –45 degrees. Then we placed one on top of the other. Your screen should look like **Figure 10.2**. Choose **Insert ➤ Convert to Symbol** and call it *Sparkle*.

■ Insert a keyframe at Frame 50. Click Frame 50 and move *Sparkle* horizontally to the right side of your screen. Select the frames and make it a motion tween.

■ Click Scene 1 to return to the main **Timeline**.

STEP 2: ADD ACTIONSCRIPT

The ActionScript controls the colors, beam length, and overall size of the firework. It also makes the fireworks twinkle and fade out.

■ Choose **Insert ➤ New Symbol**. Make it a movie clip named *firework*.

■ From the **Library** (**Window ➤ Library**) drag in an instance of *myBeam*. In the **Property inspector**, type *myBeam1* in the **Instance Name** text box.

■ Insert a layer named *actions*. Add keyframes in Frames 2 and 3. In the first keyframe, type or paste in the following ActionScript. You can find this in Frame 1 of the *firework* symbol of **10.fla**.

```
//This action script duplicates the
//symbol instance myBeam1
//and rotates it to appear as the
//firework. It randomizes the
```

```
//overall size of the firework, as
//well as the individual beam
//lengths. It also randomizes the
//color of each firework.
//Initialize variables
i=0;
//Cf is the variable that counts the
//frame and aids in setting
//the alpha value so that the
//fireworks twinkle.
cf=0;
//Number of beams regulates the
//fullness of each firework.
numberOfBeams=40;
// Random sizes are set for a single
//firework on the screen
myScale = 20 + Random(80);
//Make the instance, myBeam1,
//visible. This is necessary because
//myBeam1 gets set to invisible
//below.
setProperty("myBeam1",_visible,true)
;
// A maximum random size is set for
//the next firework on the screen
xyscalevar = 20 + Random(80);
//Randomize the color of the next
//firework
colorArray=["FF","00","33","99","66",
"CC"]
myColor=new Color(myBeam1);
myColor.setRGB("0x"+colorArray
[Random(6)]+colorArray[Random(6)]+
colorArray[Random(6)]);
// The following lines create the
//firework from a single beam
// and give each beam a random length
//which does not exceed the maximum
//size
```

```
// set by the variable xyscalevar
//above
do {
duplicateMovieClip("myBeam1","beam"
add i,i);
setProperty("beam" + i,_rotation,
random(360));
setProperty("beam" +
i,_xscale,myScale+random(myScale));
setProperty("beam" +
i,_yscale,myScale+random(myScale));
i = Number(i) + 1;
}
while (Number(i)<=numberOfBeams
)
//Make the instance, myBeam1,
//invisible. This is necessary
//because myBeam1 was never resized
//for this particular
//firework and it would look odd if
//it were visible.
setProperty("myBeam1",_visible,false
);
```

- In Frame 2, type or paste in the following ActionScript. You can find this in Frame 2 of the *firework* symbol of **10.fla**.

```
//This action script assigns the
//alpha value so that the
//fireworks twinkle. It counts the
//frames and assigns
//new alpha values depending on which
//frame the movie is in.
//Some beams do not twinkle at all.
//Increment the frame counter.
cf=cf+2;
//When the frame counter = 80, start
//a new firework.
if(cf>=80) {gotoAndPlay(1);}
```

```
//Set the new alphas for the twinkle.
//Don't twinkle until after
//the tenth frame.
if(cf>=10) {
    setProperty("beam" +
((cf/2)+1),_alpha,75);
    setProperty("beam" +
((cf/2)+2),_alpha,50);
setProperty("beam" +
    ((cf/2)+3),_alpha,25);
setProperty("beam" +
    ((cf/2)+4),_alpha,0);
setProperty("beam" +
((cf/2)+5),_alpha,25);
    setProperty("beam" +
((cf/2)+6),_alpha,50);
    setProperty("beam" +
((cf/2)+7),_alpha,75);
    setProperty("beam" +
((cf/2)+8),_alpha,100);
    setProperty("beam" +
((cf/2)+9),_alpha,75);
    setProperty("beam" +
((cf/2)+10),_alpha,50);
    setProperty("beam" +
((cf/2)+11),_alpha,25);
    setProperty("beam" +
((cf/2)+12),_alpha,0);
    setProperty("beam" +
((cf/2)+13),_alpha,25);
    setProperty("beam" +
((cf/2)+14),_alpha,50);
    setProperty("beam" +
((cf/2)+15),_alpha,75);
    setProperty("beam" +
((cf/2)+16),_alpha,100);
    setProperty("beam" + ((cf/2)-
1),_alpha,75);
    setProperty("beam" + ((cf/2)-
2),_alpha,50);
    setProperty("beam" + ((cf/2)-
3),_alpha,25);
    setProperty("beam" + ((cf/2)-
4),_alpha,0);
    setProperty("beam" + ((cf/2)-
5),_alpha,25);
    setProperty("beam" + ((cf/2)-
6),_alpha,50);
    setProperty("beam" + ((cf/2)-
7),_alpha,75);
    setProperty("beam" + ((cf/2)-
8),_alpha,100);
    setProperty("beam" + ((cf/2)-
9),_alpha,75);
    setProperty("beam" + ((cf/2)-
10),_alpha,50);
    setProperty("beam" + ((cf/2)-
11),_alpha,25);
    setProperty("beam" + ((cf/2)-
12),_alpha,0);
    setProperty("beam" + ((cf/2)-
13),_alpha,25);
    setProperty("beam" + ((cf/2)-
14),_alpha,50);
    setProperty("beam" + ((cf/2)-
15),_alpha,75);
    setProperty("beam" + ((cf/2)-
16),_alpha,100);
}
//Gradually fade the firework out in
//the last twenty frames.
//Initialize ii.
ii=0;
if (cf>=61) {
    myAlpha=100-((cf-61)*4);
    do {

if(getProperty("beam"+ii,_alpha)>=
myAlpha) {
                setProperty("beam" +
ii,_alpha,myAlpha);
        }
```

```
            ii = Number(ii) + 1;
    }
    while (Number(ii)<=numberOfBeams
    )
}
```

- In Frame 3, type or paste in the following ActionScript, which you can get from Frame 3 of the *firework* symbol of **10.fla**.

```
gotoAndPlay(2);
```

- Add a frame (**F5**) in Frame 3 of **Layer 1**.
- Click **Scene 1** to return to the main **Timeline**.

STEP 3: POSITION THE FIREWORKS

Bring the fireworks onto the main **Timeline** in different positions and at different times.

- Insert a new layer and call it *actions*. Rename Layer 1 to *fireworks*.
- On the *fireworks* layer, click Frame 1. Drag in an instance of *firework*.

- Insert keyframes in Frames 8, 14, 24, and 36 (the exact frame numbers are not important). Click each keyframe and drag in an instance of *firework* to a different location on the Stage.
- Insert a frame two frames after the last keyframe (which would be Frame 38 in our example).
- On the *actions* layer, insert a keyframe in Frame 38 (the same last frame number of the *fireworks* layer). Type or paste in the following ActionScript:

```
gotoAndPlay(37);
```

- Choose **Edit ≻ Document**. Change the background to black and change the frame rate to 24 frames per second.

Test the movie and celebrate!

CHAPTER 2

3D ANIMATION

Although Flash is a 2D program, you can make your animations look 3D within Flash. If you have access to a 3D program, by all means, use it and then import your artwork. In this chapter, we offer you techniques that don't require anything but Flash. These tricks make you think that you're seeing a three-dimensional animation.

Technique 11 is a 3D rotating logo. The effect of rotation is a common 3D technique. Technique 12 is a rotating earth. It's not as nice as those NASA photos, but it is still pretty.

ROTATING 3D LOGO

11.1

Y ou can make a logo look three-dimensional in Flash or use a logo that has been created in 3D drawing software. Then you use simple two-dimensional techniques to make it look like it's rotating.

STEP 1: CREATE THE LOGO

Import the logo (or draw it in Flash) and add the three-dimensional background.

- Usually the logo is a bitmap. Choose **File** ➢ **Import** to import it. You can also draw a logo using Flash drawing tools. If you use the **Text** tool, select the text and choose **Modify** ➢ **Break** Apart twice to turn the text into a shape.
- Select the logo, choose **Insert** ➢ **Convert to Symbol**, choose **Movie Clip Behavior**, and name it *logo*.

■ Double-click *logo* to edit it. Change the name of **Layer 1** to *logo*. Insert a new layer and name it *background*. Drag *background* below *logo*.

■ Select and copy the logo to the **Clipboard**. Lock the *logo* layer. Click Frame 2 of the *background* layer and insert a keyframe (**F6**). Paste the copy of the logo back onto the **Stage**. If the logo is a bitmap, choose **Modify ➤ Trace Bitmap**. If the logo is a vector, choose **Modify ➤ Break Apart**.

■ Use the **Paint Brush** tool to change the color of the fill of the background. Use gray for a shadow effect or a color that contrasts with the logo.

■ Place the background behind your logo. If the background shows at all, use the **Free Transform** tool to make it slightly smaller. You can also choose **Modify ➤ Transform ➤ Scale and Rotate** for more precision.

STEP 2: CREATE THE ROTATION EFFECT

With each keyframe, you expand the background and contract the logo.

■ Add a keyframe in Frame 2 of the *logo* layer and hide it.

■ Select the background and press the right arrow key a couple of times to move the background to the right. Display the *logo* layer to check if you like the result. (Depending on the shape of the logo, you may need to draw horizontal lines that appear to connect the background to the logo at the top and the bottom. Then fill in any empty area.)

■ Add a keyframe to Frame 3 of both layers. Lock the *background* layer. Use the **Free Transform** tool to make *logo* slightly narrower. Lock the *logo* layer. Move the background further to the right. Again,

fill in any empty space at the top and bottom of the logo by extending horizontal lines.

■ Add a keyframe to Frame 4 of both layers and repeat the process you did for Frame 3. But this time, also make *background* narrower. You may also want to move it slightly higher, as shown in **Figure 11.2**. Repeat for Frames 5 and 6.

■ Add keyframes to both layers of Frame 7. By now, you should have a very narrow background. You may need to make manual adjustments, especially if you have added horizontal line, as mentioned earlier. This is the side view, so you should delete *logo* completely in this keyframe. Unlock both frames.

STEP 3: COMPLETE THE ROTATION

Copy the animation to the next group of frames to double it. Then reverse the animation and flip each frame horizontally to complete the rotation.

■ Select the *logo* layer and choose **Edit ➤ Copy Frames**. Add a keyframe in Frame 8, click in FrameFrame 8 of the *logo* layer, and choose **Edit ➤ Paste Frames**. With the frames still selected, choose

11.2

Modify ➢ Frames ➢ Reverse. Do the same for the *background* layer.

■ Because Frame 8 is the same as Frame 7, right-click (Win)/Ctrl-click (Mac) Frame 8 in both layers and choose **Remove Frame**.

■ Select each frame in both layers (for example, click Frame 8 on the *logo* layer, press **Shift**, and click Frame 8 on the *background* layer). Choose **Modify ➢ Transform ➢ Flip Horizontal**. This completes the rotation of the logo.

■ Play the animation. You'll probably have to make some manual adjustments, such as by adding horizontal lines to connect the logo and the background in the second half of the animation.

■ When you're done, click **Scene 1** to return to the main **Timeline**.

■ Drag *logo* onto the **Stage** from the **Library** (**Window ➢ Library**).

Test the movie to see your logo rotate.

ROTATING EARTH

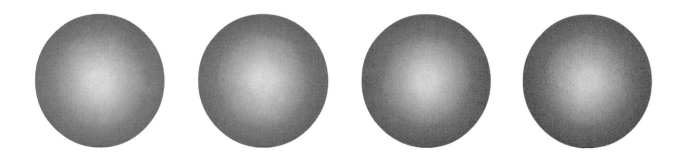

12.1 (CP 9)

R ound and round and round she goes. A rotating earth is a stunning animation and provides so many positive connotations — "We're international," "The World is My Family," We're good for the Earth," and so on. This animation is a true trompe l'oeil because it is created with 2D effects only.

STEP 1: IMPORT THE MAP

You need to start with a map and duplicate it so you have two maps side-by-side.

■ Start with a new movie. We found a map with a blue background and put the two together in Photoshop. But you can do it all in Flash:

   ■ Import a bitmap of a world map. Choose **Modify** ➤ **Trace Bitmap**. If necessary, delete any extraneous parts of the image. You want only the map.

NOTE

To see our globe, look for **12.fla** in the Techniques folder of the CD-ROM.

■ Select the map, copy it to the **Clipboard** and then paste it onto the **Stage**. Position the two side-by-side as exactly as possible. Select both copies of the map.

■ Choose **Insert ➢ Convert to Symbol**. Make it a movie clip named *earth.*

■ Double-click *earth* to edit it and add another layer. Name the two layers *map* and *water.*

■ On the *water* layer (the bottom layer), add a blue rectangle. Pay attention to the width of the rectangle, because it defines the width of the Pacific Ocean. After you have completed the motion tween, you'll have a better idea of how wide the rectangle should be, and you can go back and change its width by editing the *earth* symbol. (Our movie doesn't have this layer, because we imported both the map and the water from Photoshop.)

Click **Scene 1** to return to main **Timeline**.

STEP 2: CREATE THE EARTH

In the beginning, you get to create the earth.

■ Insert two additional layers. Name the three layers from the top down *mask, earth,* and *background.*

TIP

To test the proper size of the circle, right-click (Win)/Ctrl-click (Mac) the *mask* layer and choose Mask. Test your movie and see how it looks. If necessary, adjust the size of the circle.

■ Drag the map (the *earth* symbol) onto the *earth* layer. Select the map and choose **Alpha** from the **Color** drop-down list of the **Property inspector** (**Window ➢ Properties**). Set the **Alpha** to **50**.

■ On the *mask* layer, draw a circle with no stroke the size of the earth for your map. Position the circle over the right side of the map.

■ Select and copy the circle. Click the *background* layer and choose **Edit ➢ Paste in Place**. Lock and hide the other two layers and select the circle on the *background* layer. Open the **Color Mixer** (**Window ➢ Color Mixer** and choose **Radial** from the **Fill Style** drop-down list. Create a gradient that is white at the center and black at the outside, as shown in **Figure 12.2**. This gradient creates the impression of a 3D sphere.

STEP 3: CREATE THE MOTION TWEEN

Tween the map to move across the **Stage**.

12.2

- On the *earth* layer, insert a keyframe (**F6**) at Frame 40. (Use an earlier frame to make the earth turn faster.) Select Frames 1 through 40 and choose **Motion** from the **Tween** drop-down list of the **Property inspector**.
- Press **Shift** to keep the map from moving up or down and drag it to the right until the map on the left is exactly on top of the map on the right.
- Since Frames 1 and 40 are exactly the same, you need to delete Frame 40 so that your rotating earth does not seem to pause. To do this, create a keyframe in Frame 39 and delete Frame 40.

- Add frames (**F5**) to the *mask* and *background* frames in the same frame that your tween ends.
- If you haven't already done so, create the mask. Right-click (Win)/Ctrl-click (Mac) the *mask* layer and choose **Mask**.

Test your movie and watch as the world turns.

TEXT

Text is a very important part of your Web site, assuming that you want to say something that you can't say in pictures alone. Text animation needs to be done with forethought, because the text needs to be legible. You can probably make text glow slightly without losing too much legibility, but you probably shouldn't fully animate text that you actually want people to *read*. In most Flash sites, text is animated to create a visual effect only. So think of your text as an image and have fun with it!

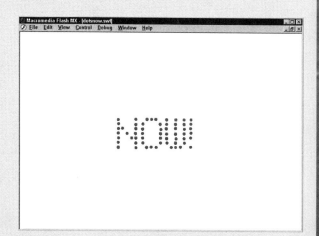

TEXT CONTROLLING OBJECTS

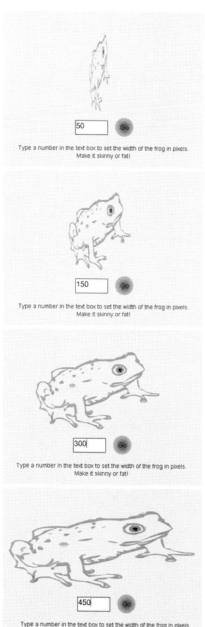

13.1

Although most text is *static,* meaning that it doesn't interact, you can also create *input* text. Input text is text that your viewers type in their browser. You can manipulate that text in many ways, using ActionScript. In this technique, you use the value that a user types in a text box to change the properties of an object. We use the width of the object in our example, but you can change any property in this way.

STEP 1: CREATE A SYMBOL

First you create an instance of a symbol with an instance name.

■ Start with a new movie and create any image on the Stage. Choose **Insert ➤ Convert to Symbol**. Make it a movie clip, name it *changeMe,* and click **OK**.

- In the **Instance Name** text box of the **Property inspector** (**Window ➤ Properties**), type *myChangeMe* to name the instance.

STEP 2: ADD AN INPUT TEXT BOX

You add a text box that will function as input text.

- Choose the **Text** tool. Choose an appropriate font size.
- In the **Property inspector**, choose **Input Text** from the **Text Type** drop-down list.
- Drag out a text box on the **Stage**.
- If necessary, click the **Expand** arrow in the lower-right corner of the **Property inspector** to expand it to full size. In the **Var** text box, type *size*. This is the variable name.
- To the left of the **Var** text box is the **Show Border Around Text** button. Click this button. This makes the border of the text box visible when you publish your movie — so your viewers know where to type the text.
- To limit input to numbers only, click the **Character** button in the Property inspector. Click the **Only** button, then check Numerals (0-9) and click **Done**.

STEP 3: CREATE A BUTTON

You create a button that will transmit the value in the text box to the symbol you created.

- Choose **Insert ➤ New Symbol**. Make it a button and call it *btnSize*. Click **OK**.

- In the **Up** keyframe, draw any shape for a button.
- Add a keyframe (**F6**) in the **Over** frame. Keep the same button, modify it, or else delete it and draw a new button. Do the same in the **Down** frame.
- Add a keyframe in the **Hit** button.
- Add a new layer, *text*. Add some text on top of the button. Be sure to set it to **Static Text** in the **Text Type** drop-down list of the Property inspector. Add keyframes to the other three frames of the *text* layer.
- Click **Scene 1** to return to the main Timeline.

STEP 4: ADD ACTIONSCRIPT TO THE BUTTON

You add the ActionScript to the button so that clicking the button changes the image.

- From the **Library** (**Window ➤ Library**), drag an instance of the button onto the **Stage** next to the input text box.
- Open the **Action** panel (**Window ➤ Actions**). Click the **View Control** button and choose **Normal** mode. Choose **Actions ➤ Movie Clip Control**. Double-click **setProperty**.
- By default, the **on (release)** event for the mouse is used. To enable users to press **Enter/Return** after they type a value, select the on(release) statement, check the **Key Press** check box above the ActionScript code and press **Enter/Return** on your keyboard.

- Click the line of ActionScript that says **setProperty**. From the **Property** drop-down list, choose a property. In our example, we use the **_width** *property*.
- Click the **Target** text box. Then click the **Insert a Target Path** button just above the code. In the **Insert Target Path** dialog box, choose *myChangeMe,* the instance name of the symbol you created. Click **OK**.
- Click the **Value** text box. Type *size,* the variable name you gave to the **Input** text box. At the right of the **Value** text box, click the **Expression** check box. Your **Action** panel should look like

Figure 13.2 when the **setProperty** line of ActionScript is selected.
- Collapse or close the **Action** panel.

STEP 5: ADD INSTRUCTIONS

You need to tell users what to do. Add some text that explains that they should type the desired width of the symbol in the text box and click the button or press Enter.

Test the movie and have fun changing the width of your image.

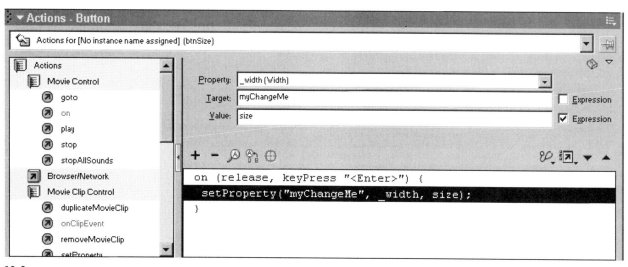

13.2

ANIMATED TEXT WARPING

14.1

Y ou can warp and manipulate text in many ways. Here we offer you two options.

FLYING LETTERS

The letters fly onto the Stage, letter by letter, first from the left and then from the right.

STEP 1: CREATE THE TEXT

You create some text and make it semitransparent.

■ Start with a new movie. Use the **Text** tool to type some text. In the **Property inspector** (**Window** ➢ **Properties**), type **100** in the **Font Size** text box.

■ Center the text horizontally on the **Stage**, so that there is an equal amount of space on the left and the right of the text. It's okay if the text goes off the **Stage**, as long as it goes off an equal amount on either side. You can eyeball this or use the **Align** panel (**Window** ➢ **Align**).

■ Open the **Color Mixer** (**Window** ➢ **Color Mixer**). Use the **Arrow** tool to select the text object. In the **Color Mixer,** change the alpha to **20%**.

■ You need to make a copy of the text for later use. Select the text and copy it to the **Clipboard**. Add a new layer (**Insert** ➢ **Layer**). Click Frame 1 of the new layer (*Layer 2*) and paste in the text. Drag the text off the **Stage**.

STEP 2: PUT EACH LETTER ON A SEPARATE LAYER

To animate the letters, each one needs to be on a separate layer. Luckily, Flash MX has two new tools that make this process easy.

■ Select the text on **Layer 1** and choose **Modify** ➢ **Break Apart**. You now see each letter as a separate object.

■ Choose **Modify** ➢ **Distribute to Layers**. As if by magic, each letter is now on its own layer, named after the letter. Delete *Layer 1*.

STEP 3: CREATE A SET OF SMALLER LETTERS

To create a sense of depth as the letters fly in, we created another set of smaller letters.

■ Drag the copy of the text you created on *Layer 2* onto the Stage. As you did with the larger text, center it horizontally on the **Stage** and place it in approximately the same vertical position as the original text.

■ Double-click to edit the text and drag across the text to select the letters. In the **Property inspector**,

set the size of the font to **61**. (Of course, the exact size is up to you.) Use the **Color Mixer** to set the alpha to **100%**.

■ Choose **Modify** ➢ **Break Apart** and then **Modify** ➢ **Distribute to Layers** to create a second set of layers each containing one letter. These layers are listed above the first set of layers.

STEP 4: MOVE THE SMALLER TEXT TO FRAME 5

You want the smaller text to fly in after the larger text appears.

■ Select all the new frames that contain the smaller letters and choose **Edit** ➢ **Cut Frames**.

■ Delete the layers that you just cut (the top set of letters) as well as **Layer 2**.

■ To select all the Frame 5s, click the top Frame 5, then scroll all the way down in the layer listing, press and hold **Shift**, and click the bottom Frame 5. Choose **Edit** ➢ **Paste Frames**.

STEP 5: CREATE THE SHAPE TWEEN

You now create a shape tween and then break apart the letters once more, this time into shapes.

■ With all the Frame 5s selected, choose **Shape** from the **Tween** drop-down list of the **Property inspector**.

■ Now select all the Frame 1s and choose **Shape** from the **Tween** drop-down list of the **Property inspector**.

■ Your shape tween is "broken" (the line in the frames of the Timeline is dashed) because the text is not fully broken apart. Click Frame 1 in each layer and choose **Ctrl+B** (Win)/⌘+**B** (Mac) to break apart the text into shapes.

■ Click Frame 5 in each layer and choose **Ctrl+B** (Win)/⌘+**B** (Mac) to break apart the text into shapes. Your shape tweens are now complete and the dashed lines in the frames of the **Timeline** become solid lines.

STEP 6: STAGGER THE LETTERS

You now want to stagger the entry of the letters so that they seem to fly in one after another.

- Select Frames 1 through 5 in the second layer (containing the second letter of your text). Drag these frames to Frame 3.
- Select Frames 1 through 5 in the third layer (containing the third letter of your text). Drag these frames to Frame 5.
- Do the same with each of the rest of the layers, dragging each one so that it starts two frames after the previous layer.

STEP 7: ADD A KEYFRAME AT THE END

Choose a frame several frames after the last frame you are using. (In our example, this is Frame 30, but it depends on how many letters you have in your text.) Select all the Frame 30s (or whatever number you chose) and insert a keyframe.

Test your movie to watch the letters fly.

GROWING LETTERS

These letters start out flat and squishy and grow up to be mature, responsible letters, with a skewing effect, as shown in **Figure 14.2**.

STEP 1: CREATE THE TEXT

Start by creating your text and making two copies of it for later.

- Start with a new movie. Use the **Text** tool to type some text.

> **NOTE**
>
> Look for **14b.fla** in the Techniques folder of the CD-ROM to see the growing letters.

- You'll need two copies later, so insert two new layers (*Layer 2* and *Layer 3*). Select Frame 1 of *Layer 1* and choose **Edit ➢ Copy Frames**. Click Frame 1 of *Layer 2* and choose **Edit ➢ Paste Frames**. Do the same for Frame 1 of *Layer 3*.

STEP 2: DISTRIBUTE THE LETTERS TO LAYERS

Put each letter on a separate layer.

- Click *Layer 1* to select it and choose **Modify ➢ Break Apart**. The words are broken up into individual letters.
- Choose **Modify ➢ Distribute to Layers**. You now have a layer for each letter, and each layer is named after the letter it contains.
- All the frames in the new layers should be selected after the **Distribute to Layers** operation. Choose **Edit ➢ Cut Frames**. Select Frame 5 on all the letter layers and insert a keyframe (**F6**). Choose **Edit ➢ Paste Frames**.
- Delete *Layer 1*.

14.2

STEP 3: SQUISH THE LETTERS

In this step, you make the letters small and fat so that they can grow.

■ Lock *Layer 2*, which contains a copy of the text.
■ Click Frame 1 of *Layer 3*, which contains another copy of the text, and press **Ctrl+B** (Win)/⌘+**B** (Mac) to break apart the words into individual letters.
■ For each letter, select the letter and use the **Free Transform** tool to make it wider (by about two to three times) and shorter (as short as possible). Reposition the letter so that it is at the bottom of the original letter (which you can see on *Layer 2*) and centered horizontally; in other words, each squished letter should be at the base of its full-size letter.

STEP 4: DISTRIBUTE THE SQUISHED LETTERS TO LAYERS

Now you want to distribute the squished letters to Frame 1 of the other distributed letters. You do this in two phases.

■ Click *Layer 3* to select all the letters and choose **Modify ➤ Distribute to Layers**. You now have a new set of distributed letters. All the frames in these new layers are selected.
■ Choose **Edit ➤ Cut Frames**. Select Frame 1 of the original letter layers (at the bottom of the layer listing), scroll down to the last letter layer, press **Shift**, and click the last letter layer. Choose **Edit ➤ Paste Frames**.
■ You now have an extra blank keyframe in Frame 5. Select all the Frame 5s in the letter layers, right-click (Win)/Ctrl-click (Mac), and choose **Clear Keyframe**.

REMINDER

To select all Frame 5s, click the top one, scroll down to the bottom one, press Shift, and click the bottom Frame 5.

■ Delete all the new letter layers (the top set) plus *Layer 2* and *Layer 3*. You should now have just one set of letter layers.

STEP 5: CREATE THE SHAPE TWEENS

You need to break apart the letters into shapes, and then you can shape tween them.

■ Select all Frame 1 keyframes and for each choose **Ctrl+B** (Win)/⌘+**B** (Mac). Do the same for all the Frame 9 keyframes.
■ Select all the layers, which automatically selects all the frames from keyframe to keyframe, and choose **Shape** from the **Tween** drop-down list of the **Property inspector** (**Window ➤ Properties**).

STEP 6: STAGGER THE TWEENS

You want the letters to sequentially grow in order, so you stagger the shape tweens.

■ Click the second layer (containing your second letter). Drag the tween two frames to the right.
■ Click each succeeding letter and drag it two more frames to the right than the previous layer. The **Timeline** should look like **Figure 14.3**.
■ Choose a frame a few frames to the right of the last keyframe. In our example, it was Frame 30, but which frame you choose depends on the length of your text. Select that frame on all the layers and choose **Insert ➤ Keyframe**.

Test your movie. Watch the letters grow.

14.3

TEXT MORPHING

15.1 (CP 10)

T his technique is one of the easiest, yet flashiest, text techniques. Text turns into an image. The secret is simply to break
the text apart into shapes, and Flash takes care of the rest.

STEP 1: CREATE THE TEXT

- Use the **Text** tool to create some text.

STEP 2: BREAK APART THE TEXT

- Choose **Modify** ➢ **Break Apart** twice (**Ctrl+B** (Win)/⌘+**B** (Mac)).

STEP 3: CREATE THE IMAGE

Here you create the image that the text will become.

- Use the Flash tools to create an image or import a bitmap image and use **Modify** ➢ **Trace Bitmap**. Make sure that your image is not a symbol or group. (If necessary, select it and choose **Modify** ➢ **Break Apart**.)

- Insert a keyframe (**F6**) in Frame 5 so that the text remains on the screen for a moment before changing shape.
- Insert a keyframe at Frame 35.
- With Frame 35 active, delete the text.

STEP 4: CREATE THE SHAPE TWEEN

Turn it all into a shape tween.

- Select all the frames from 5 through 35.
- From the **Property inspector's Tween** drop-down list, choose **Shape**. (Choose to open the **Property inspector**, if necessary.)
- If you want the tween to make the round trip back to the text again, select all the frames and choose **Edit** ➢ **Copy Frames**. Click Frame 40 and insert a keyframe (**F6**). Choose **Edit** ➢ **Paste Frames**. Select the new frames and choose **Modify** ➢ **Frames** ➢ **Reverse**.

Test the movie to see the result.

MOVIES INSIDE TEXT

Reality   Reality

Reality   Reality

16.1 (CP 11)

T he letters contain animation inside them. You create this effect by using a mask, and it's very simple, yet effective.

STEP 1: CREATE OR OPEN THE ANIMATION

We'll leave the creation of the animation up to you. You can use any of the techniques in Chapter 1, for example. We used **08.fla** — the kaleidoscope. If you are using animation from another movie, open it and save it as a new file (**File ➢ Save As**). Otherwise, just have it on-screen.

NOTE

Our example is **16.fla** in the Techniques folder of the CD-ROM.

STEP 2: ADD THE TEXT AND MAKE IT A MASK

In this step, you add text on a new layer and turn it into a mask.

- Add a new layer (**Insert ➤ Layer**). Call it *text*. It should be above your movie layer (or layers). (New layers automatically go on top.)
- Use the **Text** tool to type some text. Make it big! Use a font that has lots of space inside the letters. (See **Figure 16.1**.)

- **Right-click** (Win)/**Ctrl-click** (Mac) the **text** layer and choose **Mask** from the menu. The movie now appears inside the letters.
- Depending on the background of your original movie, you may want some contrast between the letters and the background. You can add a new layer, call it *background*, and drag it to the bottom of the layer listing. This layer will be a masked layer. Then draw a rectangle the size of the Stage with any fill color you want. (This provides a different effect from changing the Stage color of the current movie.)

Test your movie.

SWARMING DOTS FORM TEXT

17.1 (CP 12)

Dots swarm all over the screen, finally creating your text. You can change the color of the dots and make them swarm anywhere you want. As a guide, we used a font, mypager.ttf, which is made up of square dots. You can download it from www.1001freefonts.com. However, we couldn't find an equivalent for the Mac, so we made our own letters and saved them as symbols. You'll find them in the Characters folder of the Library of **17.fla**.

STEP 1: CREATE THE TEXT

If you want to download the MyPager font, go to www.1001freefonts.com. Install the font.

- Start with a new movie. If you have installed the font, use it to type your text. This technique is time-consuming if you write a lot, so keep

NOTE

You'll find the swarming dots in **17.fla** in the Techniques folder of the CD-ROM.

your text short! If you didn't install the font, choose **File ➤ Open as Library** and choose **17.fla** from the CD-ROM. Drag in the letters that you want from the Library's **Characters** folder. You can resize the font or the letters and place them wherever you want.

■ Change the layer name to *text*.

STEP 2: MAKHE DOTS

In this step, you create a symbol of a dot.

■ Add a new layer.
■ Choose the **Circle** tool. Choose a fill color with no stroke. On Frame 1 of the new layer, draw a circle that fits nicely over one of the dots of your text.
■ With the circle selected, press **F8** to convert it to a symbol. Make it a graphic symbol and call it *smalldot*.
■ Delete the circle.

NOTE

If you are using the symbols from the Library, break them apart. You can then change their fill color.

TIP

Increase the zoom to 200% or 400%. Your circle should mostly cover one of the square dots of the text.

STEP 3: MOVE THE DOTS

You want the dots to swarm around, so you create a motion tween along a path.

■ Choose **Insert ➤ New Symbol** to create a new movie clip symbol named *mydot*.
■ From the Library, drag in *smalldot* and center it on the registration point.
■ Under the layer listing, click **Add Motion Guide**.
■ On the **Motion Guide** layer, use the **Pencil** tool with the **Smooth** option to draw a swirling shape, as shown in **Figure 17.2**.
■ Drag *smalldot* so that it locks to the beginning of the motion path you drew. (You should see a small circle indicating that *smalldot* locked to the motion path.)
■ Add a keyframe at Frame 40. Add keyframes on both layers at Frame 100. Lock the guide layer and drag *smalldot* to the end of the motion path, making sure that it locks.
■ Play the animation to make sure that *smalldot* moves along the path.
■ If you want your dots to change color as they swarm and form words, select *smalldot* at Frame 40 and in the **Color** drop-down menu in the **Property inspector**, choose **Tint**. Then select whatever color you want.
■ Click **Scene 1** to return to the main **Timeline**.

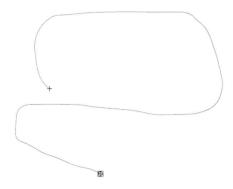

17.2

STEP 4: PLACE THE DOTS ON THE TEXT

Now you place copies of *mydot* on the dots on your text.

- Lock the *text* layer.
- Rename *Layer 2* to *dots*.
- Insert a frame at Frame 100 on both layers.
- Click Frame 1. Drag a copy of *mydot* from the **Library** onto any square dot that makes up the first letter of your text. Drag another copy of *mydot* onto any square dot of your second letter. Do the same for all the letters of your text.
- Add a keyframe (**F6**) in Frame 2. Again, drag copies of *mydot* to randomly chosen square dots of the letters of your text.
- Continue to add keyframes in each frame and drag copies of *mydot* onto the text. Because letters have different numbers of dots, in some cases, you need to drag more than one *mydot* onto a letter. You want all the letters to be completed at the same time.
- Delete the *text* layer.

Play the movie and watch the dots become the text.

> **TIP**
>
> Line up the copies of *mydot* carefully so that the final letters look straight. Use the arrow keys to move them in place after you drag them in from the Library. You may want to increase the zoom.

18

RADIATING TEXT EFFECTS

Aurora

Aurora

Aurora

18.1

Radiating, pulsing, glowing text. This technique makes text psychedelic and it's very easy to do.

STEP 1: CREATE THE TEXT

Start with a new movie. Choose your *font* and type the *text* that you want to glow. Try to choose a "fat" font with lots of thickness in the letters.

STEP 2: SOFTEN THE EDGES

First, make a symbol of the text, and then soften its edges.

- Click the first frame and choose **Edit ➢ Copy Frames**.
- Choose **Insert ➢ New Symbol**. Make it a movie clip, name it *text*, and click **OK**.

- Click the first frame and choose **Edit** ➢ **Paste Frames**.
- Break apart the text two times so it turns into shapes — **Ctrl+B** (Win)/**⌘+B** (Mac).
- Choose **Modify** ➢ **Shape** ➢ **Soften Fill Edges**. Set the distance to anywhere from about **10** to **30** pixels and the number of steps to **4**. The **Direction** should be set to **Expand**. (The numbers you use depend on the size of your text.) Click **OK**.

STEP 3: CREATE A SHAPE TWEEN

Create a shape tween that changes the alpha (opaqueness/transparency) of the text.

- Insert a keyframe (**F6**) in Frames 15 and 30.
- Open the **Color Mixer** (**Window** ➢ **Color Mixer**). Click Frame 1 and set the alpha to **5**. Click the text with the **Paint Bucket** tool. Click Frame 15, set the alpha to **15** and click the text with the **Paint Bucket** tool. Click Frame 30 , set the alpha to **5** and click the text with the **Paint Bucket** tool.

- Select Frames 1 through 30. From the Tween drop-down list of the **Property inspector**, choose **Shape** to create a shape tween.
- Click **Scene 1** to return to the main **Timeline**.

STEP 4: MAKE THE TEXT GLOW

You bring the glowing text back onto the original text.

- Create a new layer *glowText* and drag it beneath the original layer.
- From the Library (**Window** ➢ **Library**), drag in *text* onto the *glowText* layer. Place it in the same location as the original text you created.

Test your movie and watch the text glow!

NOTE

You can find our glowing text, Aurora, in the Techniques folder of the CD-ROM as **18.fla**.

4

SOUND AND VIDEO

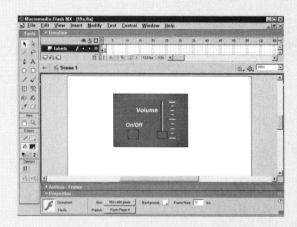

Sound can make a great addition to any Web site, but you should offer your users some control. Other people in the vicinity might not want to hear your music! Technique 19 lets users control the volume and turn the sound on and off.

Video is a new feature of Flash MX. You can now insert video files into your Flash movies. We show you how in Technique 20.

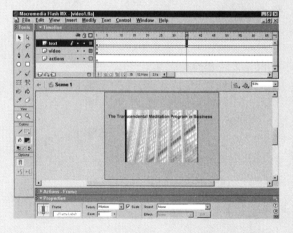

ON/OFF AND VOLUME
SOUND CONTROLS

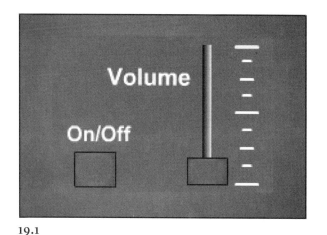

19.1

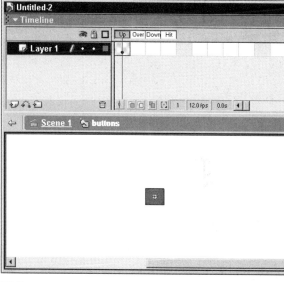

19.2

The sound button turns the sound on and off. The volume control is a slider that adjusts the volume of the sound in your movie. Consider using this technique a kindness to your viewers — and to others within earshot!

STEP 1: CREATE A BUTTON

The first step is to create a button for the on/off button and the slider.

- Choose **Insert ➤ New Symbol**. Choose **Button** as the behavior and name it *buttons*. Your screen should look like **Figure 19.2**.
- Create the graphic for the Up state in the Up frame. Make the button about 32 pixels wide.
- Add keyframes (**F6**) to the **Over, Down**, and **Hit** frames to copy the graphic to those frames. Sliders don't usually change in the Over and Down frames, but of course, your slider can be different.
- Click **Scene 1** to return to the main Timeline.

STEP 2: CREATE THE SLIDER BAR

Create the vertical bar for the slider.

- Choose **Insert** ➢ **New Symbol**. Make it a movie clip and name it *SliderBar*. Draw the slider bar. Ours is just a long, thin rectangle with a black-and-white linear gradient fill.
- Click **Scene 1** to return to the main **Timeline**.

STEP 3: ASSEMBLE THE BUTTONS AND SLIDER BAR

You bring the buttons and slider bar onto the **Stage** and add a background.

- Insert four new layers for a total of five layers. From the top, name them *labels, buttons, slider, actions,* and *background.*
- In Frame 1 of the *buttons* layer, drag two instances of *buttons* from the Library (**Window** ➢ **Library**).
- Select the instance of *buttons* that you want to be the on/off button. In the **Property inspector** (**Window** ➢ **Properties**), type *playButton* in the **Instance Name** text box.
- Select the instance of *buttons* that you want to be the slider. If you wish, use the **Free Transform** tool to make it shorter vertically, as you can see in Figure 19.1. In the **Property inspector**, type

mySlider in the **Instance Name** text box and choose **Movie Clip** from the **Symbol Behavior** drop-down list to change it to a movie clip.
- In Frame 1 of the *slider* layer, drag in an instance of *SliderBar*. Position the slider button on the bottom of the slider bar. In the **Property inspector**, type *mySliderBar* in the **Instance Name** text box.
- On the *background* layer, draw your background.
- On the *labels* layer, use the **Text** tool to label the button and the slider bar, as shown in Figure 19.1.

STEP 4: IMPORT THE SOUND

You import that sound that you want to play and configure it to be accessible to the ActionScript.

- Choose **File** ➢ **Import** and import the sound you want to play. Choose **All Sound Formats** from the **Files of Type** drop-down list, locate the sound, and click **Open**.
- **Right-click** (Win)/**Ctrl-click** (Mac) the sound in the **Library** (**Window** ➢ **Library**) and choose **Linkage**. In the **Linkage Properties** dialog box, shown in Figure 19.3, choose **Export for ActionScript**. In the **Identifier** text box, type *mySound*. Click **OK**.

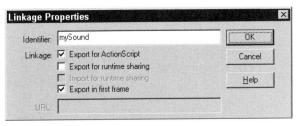

19.3

STEP 5: ADD THE ACTIONSCRIPT

Add the ActionScript to control the buttons.

■ In Frame 1 of the *actions* layer, type or paste in the following ActionScript. You can find it in Frame 1 of the *actions* layer of **19.fla**.

```
//Create an instance of the Sound
//object called "thisSound"
//and use the method "attachSound" to
//attach the sound from
//the library. Remember to link the
//sound in the library to
//export to an action script. (Right
//or Ctrl-click on the
//symbol and choose "Linkage").
thisSound = new Sound;
thisSound.attachSound("mySound");
//Initialize the soundOn variable to
//false.
soundOn=false;
```

■ In Frame 2 of the *actions* layer, insert a keyframe (**F6**) and then type or paste in the following ActionScript. You can find it in Frame 2 of the *actions* layer of **19.fla**.

```
//Stop the movie in the main
//timeline and wait for a
//button to be pushed or slided.
stop();
//playButton is the instance of the
//on/off button and
//on its release, if the sound is
//off, then it starts the
//sound playing, and sets soundOn
//to true. When the sound
//is complete, it begins again.
//thisSound is the instance of
```

```
//the sound object that was created
//in the action script in
//frame one.
playButton.onRelease =
function() {
  if (soundOn==false) {
        thisSound.start();
        soundOn=true;
        song.onSoundComplete =
function() {
              thisSound.start();
        }
//if the sound is on, while the
//button is pushed, then
//the sound stops, and soundOn is
//set to false.
  } else {
        thisSound.stop();
        soundOn=false;
  }
}
```

■ Select the slider button and type or paste in the following ActionScript. You can find this ActionScript by clicking the slider button in **19.fla**.

```
//This button is both a movie clip
//and a button, because it
//needs to respond as a button and it
//also needs to slide.
//To do this, you need to have it as
//a button in the symbol
//library, then assign it as a movie
//clip instance in the
//properties box.
onClipEvent(load){
```

```
//myY is the position of the slider
//button
//the button must be positioned at
//the bottom
//of the slider to start
    myY=_y;
//the top of the slider bar is top
    top=_y-
_root.mySliderBar._height;
//the bottom of the slider bar is
//bottom, and it
//is set by the position of the
//button, which must
//be placed at the bottom.
    bottom= _y;
//right and left are the _x position
//of the button
//(the middle of the button)
    right=_x;
    left=_x;
//set the volume to off.
//thisSound is created in the
//action script in frame one, and
//needs to be targeted
//by using the word "_root" in front
//of it.
    _root.thisSound.setVolume(0);
}


//The following lines allow the
//button/movie clip to be
//dragged, but only up and down and
//only for the
//height of the slider. Left and
//right are set to the
```

```
//same value, so it cannot go left or
//right, only up and down.
on(press){

startDrag("",false,left,top,right,
bottom);
}
on(release){
    stopDrag();
//The volume is a number between
//zero and 100 and
//represents the difference
//between the bottom of
//the slider and the current
//position of the button
//times the ratio of the full
//volume (100) to the
//height of the slider bar.
//This gives a value of
//100 when the slider button
//is at the top of the
//slider bar, and adjusts the
//volume correctly for
//every position in between
//the top and the bottom.
    _root.thisSound.setVolume((myY-
_y)*100/_root.mySliderBar._height);
    }
```

■ Select Frame 2 in the other layers and add a frame (**F5**).

Test the movie. Move the Volume slider up and click the On/Off button.

ADDING VIDEO TO A FLASH MOVIE

20.1

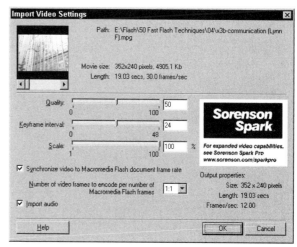

20.2

S upport for video is a new feature of Flash MX. If you have QuickTime 4 installed on your Mac or PC, you can import files in the AVI, MPG/MPEG, MOV, and DV formats. If you have DirectX 7 or higher installed on your PC, you can import files in the AVI, MPG/MPEG, and Windows Media File (WMV and ASF) formats.

STEP 1: IMPORT THE VIDEO FILE

First you import the video file and specify settings for the file.

- Click a keyframe. (Press **F6** to create one if necessary.)
- Choose **File ➢ Import** to open the **Import** dialog box. Choose a video file and click **Import**. The **Import Video Settings** dialog box appears, shown in **Figure 20.2**.

STEP 2: SPECIFY THE VIDEO SETTINGS

In the **Import Video Settings** dialog box, you make all-important decisions about the quality and size of your video.

- Drag the **Quality** slider to choose the amount of compression. Less compression means higher-quality video but a larger file size.
- Drag the **Keyframe Interval** slider to choose the frequency of keyframes in the video clip. A keyframe stores the entire picture data for that frame, while the other frames store only the changes from the previous frame. Fewer keyframes means smaller files.
- Drag the **Scale** slider to adjust the pixel dimensions of the movie. Settings at less than 100% make a smaller movie, which may play more smoothly.
- Choose **Synchronize Video to Macromedia Flash Movie Frame Rate** if you want the video clip frame rate to match the frame rate of your Flash movie. Usually, you want to choose this option. Sometimes, however, you may not want to choose it, if, for example, your Flash movie has a lower frame rate than your video clip and you want to avoid dropping frames from your video clip.

- Choose a ratio from the **Number of Video Frames to Encode Per Number of Flash Frames** drop-down list. If you choose 1:1, your movie plays one imported video frame for each Flash frame in your main Timeline. If you choose 1:2, your movie plays on imported video frame for every two Flash frames, and so on. As you drop from your video clip, your file is smaller; however, playback may be less smooth.
- Choose **Import Audio** if you want to include the audio (if any) from the video clip you are importing. Flash can't import the audio from your video clip if the audio is compressed using a software format not available on your computer. (If that's the case, Flash warns you after you click OK.)
- Click **OK**. If your video clip is longer than the span between keyframes into which you are placing the clip, a dialog appears asking if you want to add to the span the number of frames required to play the entire clip. Click **yes** if you want to add the frames. The video clip will stop playing at the end of the span. If you chose **no**, later on you can still move the keyframe at the end of the span to add more frames.

Test your movie to watch the video. You can scale, rotate, and tween your video clip.

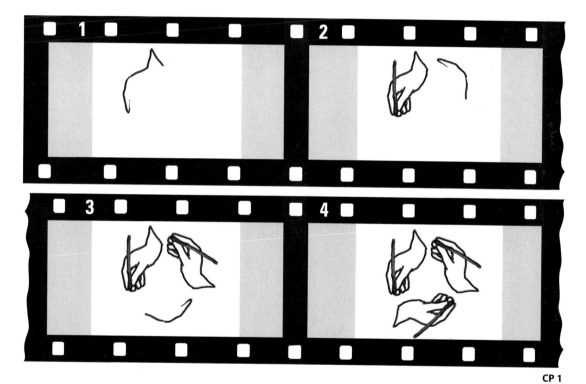

CP 1

Technique 1: A Line Drawing Itself

A common technique is to let your graphics sequentially unfold, seeming to draw themselves. We offer two ways of accomplishing this technique, which are both easy. Here you see a hand drawing itself.

CP 2

Technique 2: Make a character walk

Flash is a great tool for creating cartoons, but you need to know the specialized techniques. Our astronaut bounces a little more than most people, due to the low gravity.

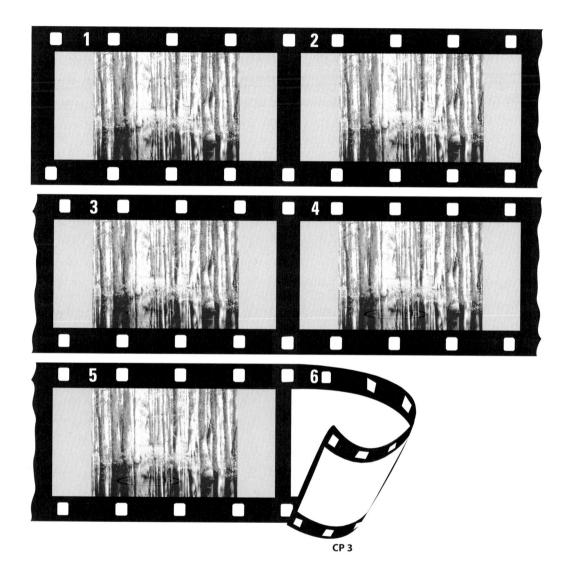

CP 3

Technique 4: Photographic ripple effects

You can make a photograph seem to come alive by animating it. One possibility is concentric ripples from an imaginary stone thrown in a pond. The ripples look like they are part of the photograph as they travel outward and disappear.

CP 4

Technique 5: Dissolve vector graphic into a bitmap

Blurring the distinction between vector graphics and bitmap photographs plays with your mind a little. Start with a photo and use the Trace Bitmap feature to convert it to a vector. Then create two tweens to gradually fade out the vector image and fade in the photo.

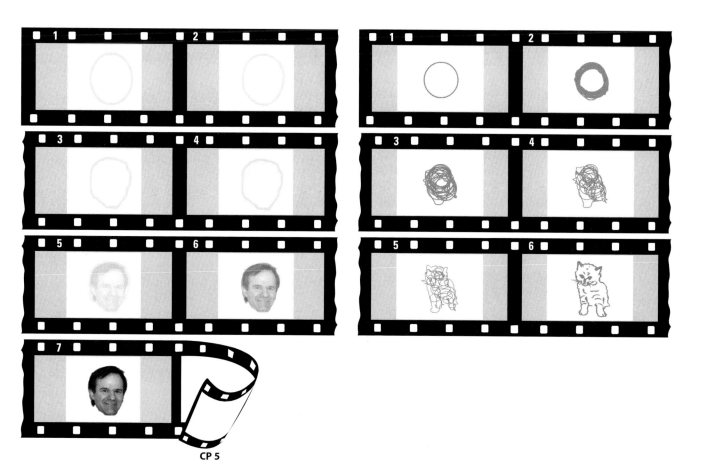

Technique 6: Morph a geometric shape into a graphic image

Shape tweening (morphing) is easy, but impressive. We turn a circle into a photograph of a face and a drawing of a cat. Turning a circle into a photograph involves a simple alpha (transparency) tween as well.

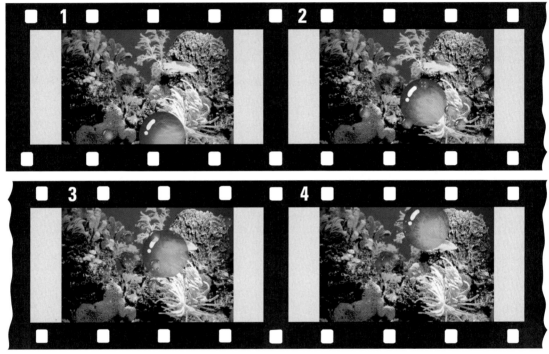

CP 6

Technique 7: Animated bubbles

These bubbles rise in a tropical underwater setting and then burst near the surface. You can use bubbles wherever there is water. By creating symbols that contain several bubbles and then inserting several instances of the symbols, you can quickly build up an impressive display of bubbles.

Technique 8: Kaleidoscope

You never know what shapes will appear in a kaleidoscope—that's why it's so fascinating. This kaleidoscope provides endless variations of shape and color.

CP 8

Technique 9: Warping images

You can warp and reshape an image in many ways, and we offer you three. Two are warped using ActionScript to warp the image horizontally and vertically, and the third is warped using just the Free Transform tool. Here you see the third warping method.

CP 9

Technique 12: Rotating 3D Globe

The earth rotates as we learned in school, and here we show it to you in brilliant color. It's very pretty. Ours is large, but you can make it much smaller if you want.

CP 10

Technique 15: Text morphing

You can turn any text into any shape using shape tweening. The secret is to break apart the text twice so that it turns into shapes. Here we take the word, "star" and turn it into a star.

Technique 16: Movies inside of text

Make your text more exciting by animating the inside of the letters. We took our kaleidoscope animation (Technique 8) and filled text with it, for a very dynamic "Reality" statement.

CP 12

Technique 17: Swarming dots form text

A swarm of dots flies around the Stage and then coalesces into a word. You don't know what the word will be until it happens. Anticipation!

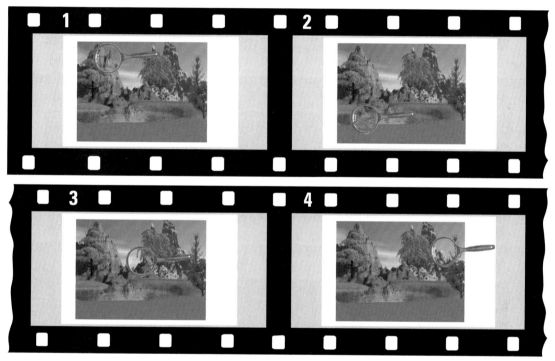

Technique 21: Draggable magnifying lens

When you move a real magnifying lens over an object, only the portion of the object under the lens is magnified. The same happens with our draggable magnifying lens. Viewers can magnify the portion of the image that interests them.

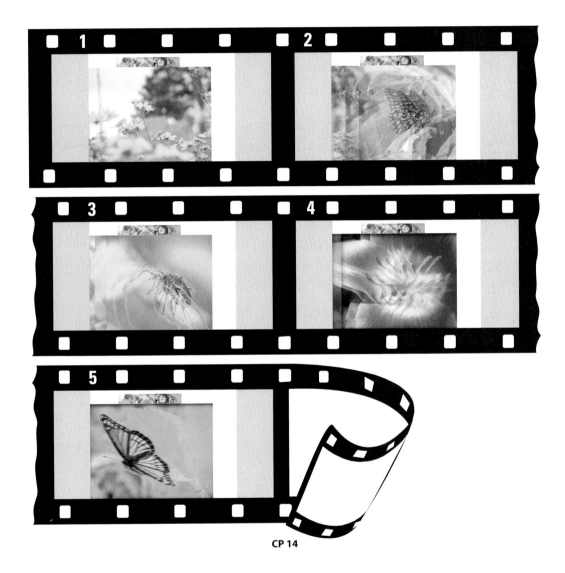

CP 14

Technique 23: Image slide scroller with motion blur

An image slide scroller is a striking way to display a portfolio of art or let viewers choose from any set of items. The viewers click a button to choose the item they want to see, and the images scroll past in a blur before slowing down and becoming crystal clear.

CP 15

Technique 24: Pan and zoom an image

Buttons on the screen let users zoom in and out to see an image closer in or farther out. Placing the cursor on either side of the screen pans (scrolls) the image left or right. Interactive techniques such as this involve people more directly with your site.

CP 16

Technique 25: Make a scrolling virtual reality panorama

Create a 360-degree panoramic scene, and let viewers scroll all the way around it. They go for a virtual walk through your imaginary world.

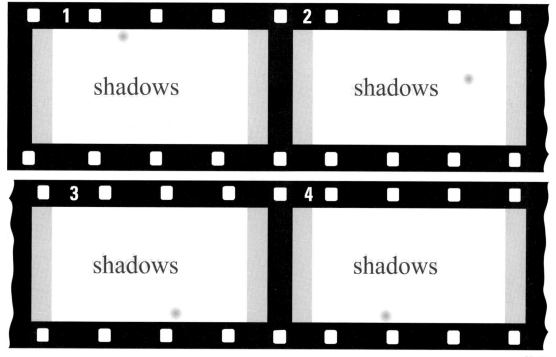

CP 17

Technique 27: Interactive shadows

As you move the cursor around the words, the shadows move to the opposite side, as if your cursor is a light and the letters are casting the shadows. Playing around with this type of interactivity is addictive!

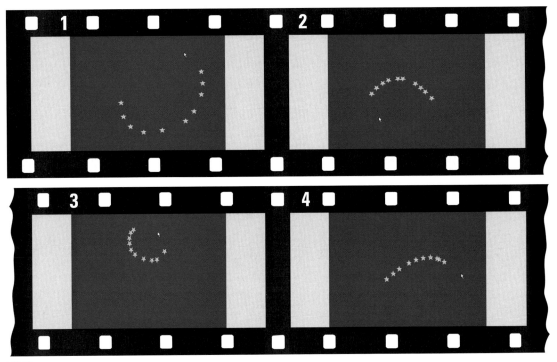

CP 18

Technique 28: Mouse trails

Mouse trails are any graphics that follow your mouse cursor. You can make lovely patterns by quickly swirling the mouse around the screen. We use stars against a blue background, but you could just as easily put butterflies against a flowery background or anything else you can conjure up.

Technique 29: Tabbed folders

Tabbed folders are an effective way to provide viewers with easy-to-use menu choices. Tabs are very common, so people immediately understand how to use them. Our example offers a site that sells used textbooks and each tab presents an academic subject.

CP 20

Technique 30: Scroll bars

When you don't have enough room to display all your text, you can place the text inside a box that scrolls. Readers use the vertical scroll bar to scroll down and read all the text. Here you see two scroll bars—one that lets users choose a course and the second that displays a description of the selected course.

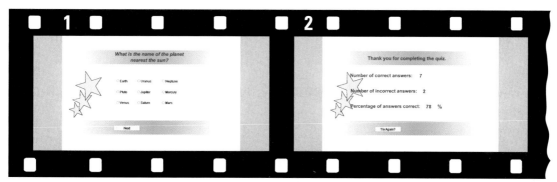

CP 21

Technique 32: Multiple choice quiz

Test your viewers knowledge with a multiple choice or True/False quiz. Then give them their score and let them take the quiz again if they want.

CP 22

Technique 35: Collapsible list

Another menu technique is the collapsible list. Clicking an item opens up a submenu. We made ours beautiful because it's about permaculture—the art and science of creating permanent landscapes for food, beauty, and the sustainability of the local ecosystem.

art by Dale Divoky

CP 23

Technique 36: 3D book as a user interface

Instead of clicking buttons to view pages, why not let users flip through a book? Actually, the pages are buttons, but the book provides an enjoyable way to look at a series of artistic creations. The 3D book can be used as a mechanism for a slide show.

CP 24

Technique 40: Animated buttons

This cute button is an apple that gets eaten up as you place the mouse cursor over it, with sound effects to match. It's a plaything, but can also function as a typical button. Buttons can rotate, pulsate, or morph—anything for a more interesting interface!

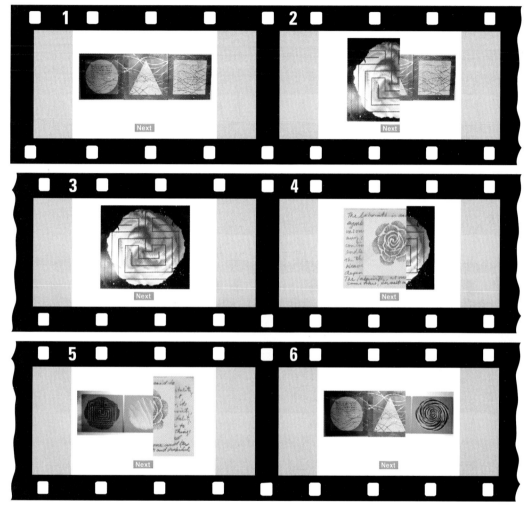

Technique 42: Slide show with special effects transitions

Flash is often used for slide shows, and we offer two special effects for the transitions between the slides—a dissolve and a wipe. Here you see the wipe for a slide show of fine art.

CP 26

Technique 43: News ticker

A news ticker streams text across the screen. From tradition, users know it must be important! You can stream text from any source across your Web page. We use an outside text file.

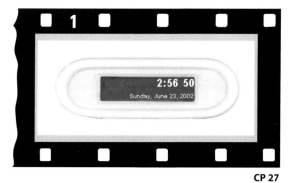

CP 27

Technique 44: Analog or digital clock

You can add a clock to your site, one much prettier than the time/date function normally available on your computer. We've created both analog (with hands) and digital (without hands) clocks.

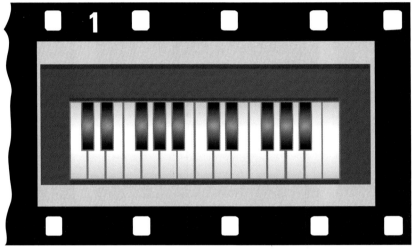

CP 28

Technique 45: Music keyboard and synthesizer

Let your viewers play the piano for fun or as a learning tool. They can use the computer keys as if they were piano keys or click with the mouse. We provided two octaves, but you can create more if you're ambitious.

CP 29

Technique 46: MP3 player

Play your MP3 music using this MP3 player. You can start, stop, and rewind.
You can turn it up higher and higher....

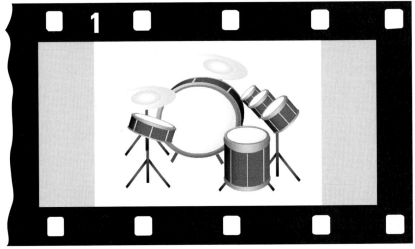

CP 30

Technique 47: Drum set

Your viewers will love playing around with our drum set. Just pass the mouse cursor over the drums and cymbals and you'll sound like a pro. You can create as many drums and sounds as you want. Kids and teens will love it.

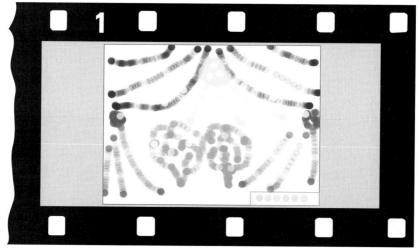

Technique 48: On-screen paint program

Our on-screen paint program is just for fun. You can change the shape that is painted onto the Stage and get different effects by placing one color on top of another.

CP 32

Technique 49: Calculator

The calculator is useful and educational as well. You might not want to do your taxes with it, but a calculator can be a great addition to a Web site.

CHAPTER 5

INTERACTIVE EFFECTS

When you use interactive effects on your site, you engage your viewers. They participate in an experience. Most interactive effects involve the users manipulating what they see on the screen in some way.

In Technique 21, users drag a magnifying lens around the screen, which magnifies the image beneath the lens. Technique 22 creates draggable movies. The movie can be any animation you want. Technique 23 is a scrollable slide show, with an added twist — the images blur for a second before becoming crystal clear. Use Technique 24 to enable viewers to control what they see — they can pan anywhere in an image and zoom in or out. In Technique 25, you create a 360-degree panorama and viewers can scroll anywhere throughout the image. Technique 26 creates a draggable mask. A mask is a "window" that displays whatever is beneath the mask. As your viewers drag the mask, they uncover different areas of an image. The last technique, Technique 27, creates interactive shadows. As you move the cursor, the shadows move in the opposite direction.

DRAGGABLE MAGNIFYING LENS

21.1 (CP 13)

The viewer drags a magnifying lens around the screen, and whatever is beneath it is magnified.

STEP 1: DRAW THE MAGNIFYING GLASS

First, you draw a magnifying glass as a button symbol.

■ Start with a new movie. Choose **Insert** ➤ **New Symbol**. Make it a button and name it *magnifier*.

■ Draw a magnifying glass in the **Up** frame. You don't need to add keyframes for the other frames, but you can if you want. All four frames should be the same.

■ Click **Scene 1** to return to the main Timeline.

NOTE

Look for our magnifying lens, **21.fla**, in the Techniques folder of the CD-ROM.

STEP 2: IMPORT AN IMAGE TO MAGNIFY

Import a nice scene or photo.

- Choose **File** ➢ **Import** and import any photo or scene that you want to magnify.
- Choose **Insert** ➢ **Convert to Symbol**. Make it a movie clip named *pic*.

STEP 3: CREATE THE MAGNIFIED IMAGE

Here you scale the image to twice its original size.

- Choose **Insert** ➢ **New Symbol**. Make it a movie clip named *bigPic*.
- Drag *pic* onto the Stage and center it.
- Choose **Modify** ➢ **Transform** ➢ **Scale and Rotate** and scale it to **200%**. Click **OK**.
- Click **Scene 1** to return to the main **Timeline**.

STEP 4: MAKE THE MAGNIFYING GLASS DRAGGABLE

You put the Magnifier button inside a movie clip and make it draggable.

- Choose **Insert** ➢ **New Symbol**. Make a movie clip named *myMagnifier*.
- Rename **Layer 1** to *magnifier*. Click Frame 1. From the **Library** (**Window** ➢ **Library**), drag in *magnifier*.
- With *magnifier* selected, open (**Window** ➢ **Actions**) or expand the **Actions** panel. Click the **View Control** button and choose **Normal** mode.

- Choose **Actions** ➢ **Movie Clip Control** and double-click **startDrag**. Select the first line of ActionScript. In the **Event** checkboxes, uncheck **Release** and check **Press**.
- Select the last line of **ActionScript** (the closing curly bracket). From the **Movie Clip Control** section of the menu, double-click **stopDrag**.
- Close or collapse the **Actions** panel.
- Insert a new layer and name it *mask*. On the *mask* layer, draw a circle with no stroke. The circle should be the same size as the lens of the magnifying glass. Center the circle over the lens of the magnifying glass.
- Insert a new layer and name it *bigPic*. Drag it to the bottom of the list. Drag in *bigPic* from the Library. Select *bigPic* and open or expand the Property inspector. Type *bigPic* in the **Instance Name** text box. This instance name is used in the ActionScript.
- **Right-click** (Win)/**Ctrl-click** (Mac) the *mask* layer and choose **Mask** from the menu to make the layer a mask.
- Click **Scene 1** to return to the main Timeline.

STEP 5: BRING IN THE SCENE AND ADD ACTIONSCRIPT

You assemble the movie and add ActionScript to create the magnifying effect.

- Rename **Layer 1** to *smallPic*. Lock this layer by clicking its **Lock** icon. Add a new layer and name it *magnifier*.
- From the **Library**, drag *myMagnifier* onto the **Stage**. It is important that *myMagnifier* be perfectly centered over the original picture because it contains the magnified picture. You can use the Align panel (**Window** ➢ **Align**) or use the X, Y text boxes of the Property inspector.
- Select *myMagnifier* and open (**Window** ➢ **Actions**) or expand the **Actions** panel. Type or paste the following ActionScript:

```
onClipEvent(load) {
//enter the value which you scaled
//your bigPic for
//the magnification (e.g. 1.5=150%)
magnification=2;
lastX=_x;
lastY=_y;
}
onClipEvent(enterFrame) {
//find out how much the magnifier has
//moved and
//multiply the distance by the
//magnification
bigPicMoveX=(lastX-_x)
*magnification;
bigPicMoveY=(lastY-_y)
*magnification;
//remember where the magnifier was
//for next move
lastX=_x;
lastY=_y;
//move the location of bigPic which
//is under the mask
bigPic._x=bigPic._x+bigPicMoveX;
bigPic._y=bigPic._y+bigPicMoveY;
}
```

Test your movie and drag the magnifying glass around to see the magnification.

DRAGGABLE MOVIES

22.1

In this technique, you place a small animation in a box, and the viewer can drag the box around while the animation continues.

STEP 1: PREPARE YOUR MOVIE AS A SYMBOL

You can create a Flash movie containing basic animation just for the purpose of this technique or use an existing movie. Either way, it all needs to be contained in a movie clip symbol. If you're creating animation just for this purpose, you can insert a new symbol (**Insert** ➤ **New Symbol**), make it a movie clip, and create the movie. To use an existing movie, you need to convert all the content on the Timeline to a symbol:

91

> **NOTE**
>
> You can find our draggable movie as **22a.fla** in the Techniques folder of the CD-ROM.

- Open the movie, choose **File** ➢ **Save As**, and save it under a new name.
- Select all the frames.
- Choose **Edit** ➢ **Copy Frames**.
- Choose **Insert** ➢ **New Symbol**. Make it a movie clip. Name it *wholething*.
- Click the first frame of the symbol and choose **Edit** ➢ **Paste Frames**.
- Click **Scene 1** to return to the main Timeline.
- Select all the frames, **right-click** (Win)/ **Ctrl-click** (Mac), and choose **Clear Frames**.
- Delete all the layers except one. (You must leave at least one layer.)

STEP 2: RESIZE THE MOVIE CLIP

You probably want your movie to be fairly small. In our example, we made it 100 x 100 pixels.

- Double-click *wholething* in the **Library** (**Window** ➢ **Library**) to edit it.
- Select the symbol and open the **Property inspector** (**Window** ➢ **Properties**).
- In the **Property inspector**, type **100** in both the X and Y text boxes to resize the symbol.
- Choose **Scene 1** to return to the main **Timeline**.

STEP 3: MAKE A BUTTON

To make an object draggable, you need a button inside a movie clip. Here you create the button.

- Choose **Insert** ➢ **New Symbol**, choose the **Button** behavior, and name it *frame*.
- Draw a rectangle and drag it so that it's centered over the registration point. We made ours

110 x 110 pixels (using the **X** and **Y** text boxes in the Property inspector). We also made the stroke 6 pixels wide. Select the fill, open the **Color Mixer** (**Window** ➢ **Color Mixer**), and change the alpha of the fill to **0**.

- Add keyframes to the other frames of the button.
- Choose **Scene 1** to return to the main **Timeline**.

STEP 4: MAKE A MOVIE CLIP

Now you add the movie clip.

- Choose **Insert** ➢ **New Symbol**. Make it a movie clip and call it *draggableMovie*.

> ### RESIZING A FLASH MOVIE
>
> **I**f your movie is complex, you can't always just resize it using the Property inspector—you may not affect the movie on all the frames. Here is another technique for rescaling a movie. Decide the reduction you want to achieve by looking at the current size of the movie in the Property inspector. Unlock and unhide all layers. Click Edit Multiple Frames (just below the Timeline) and drag the onion skin markers that appear above the Timeline to the beginning and ending frames of the animation. Choose Edit ➢ Select all and multiply all the numbers in the H, W, X & Y text boxes by the reduction amount (such as 25%). In any event, play the movie to see if it all works properly.

> **NOTE**
>
> To create a draggable movie without a frame, delete the frame, leaving just the transparent fill. You can see the version without the frame in **22b.fla** in the Techniques folder of the CD-ROM. See **Figure 22.2**.

- Change the name of your layer to *movie.* Drag *wholething* from the **Library** onto Frame 1 of the *movie* layer.
- Add a new layer and name it *frame.* Drag the *frame* symbol onto Frame 1 of the *frame* layer.
- Center the frame around the movie.
- With the **frame** symbol selected, open the **Actions** panel (**Window** ➢ **Actions**). Click the **View Control** button and choose **Normal** mode.
- In the menu on the left, click **Actions** ➢ **Movie Clip Control**, and double-click **startDrag**. Select the top line of ActionScript. In the top area of the panel, uncheck **Release** and check **Press** so that the dragging starts when you press the mouse button.
- Click the last line of code (the last curly brace) and double-click **stopDrag** from the **Movie Clip**

Control menu. Your code should now look like this:

```
on(press)}
    startDrag("");
}
on(release)
    stopDrag();
```

- Close or hide the **Actions** panel.
- Click **Scene 1** to return to the main Timeline.

STEP 5: INSERT THE DRAGGABLE MOVIE

- Drag the *draggableMovie* symbol onto Frame 1 of your main **Timeline**.

Test the movie and drag it around the screen.

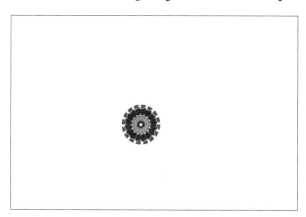

22.2

IMAGE SLIDE SCROLLER WITH MOTION BLUR

 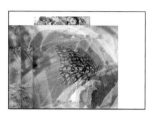 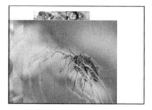

 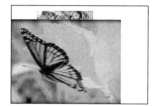

23.1 (CP 14)

The viewer clicks on a button, and an image scrolls to the center of the screen with a blurred effect as it moves. This technique is great for letting viewers view a close-up of an image or scan through a portfolio.

STEP 1: CREATE THE FILMSTRIP

You import or create the images for the scroller and place them side-by-side as in a filmstrip.

■ Start with a new movie. Choose **File** ➤ **Import** and import the images for the scroller. They should all be the same size. Delete them from the **Stage** — they're in the **Library**.

■ Drag each image individually from the Library (**Window** ➤ **Library**) and choose **Modify** ➤ **Transform** ➤ **Scale and Rotate**. Scale each one to **10%**. The exact size will depend on the size of your large images and how many you need to fit on the Stage. These small images will function as buttons, but for now, they're just images.

■ Place the small images side by side. Use the **Align** panel (**Window** ➢ **Align**) to align them. Place them where you want the buttons to go.

STEP 2: CREATE THE BUTTONS

Now you create buttons and place them over the small filmstrip.

■ Insert a new layer and name it *buttons.* Draw a rectangle that has no stroke. Make sure that the color fill is different from the background. (At the end, you'll change the fill to match the background.) Make the rectangle the same size as one of the small images.

■ With the rectangle selected, choose **Insert** ➢ **Convert to Symbol**, make it a button, and name it *whitebutton.* (In our example, the Stage is white, and the button will later be changed to white.)

■ Copy and paste the button and place it over the next small image. Do this for all the images.

■ Select each button in turn, open (**Window** ➢ **Actions**) or expand the **Actions** panel, and type or paste the following ActionScript. The number after "picno=" must change with each button, so that the rightmost is **1** and the leftmost is the number of buttons you have (**5** in our example).

To size the rectangle, select one of the small images and check its size in the H and W text boxes of the Property inspector (**Window** ➢ **Properties**). Then select the rectangle and type in the same values. You can also use the Match Size button in the Align panel (**Window** ➢ **Align**).

NOTE

Find our image scroller in the Techniques folder of the CD-ROM — look for **23.fla.**

```
on (press) {
with (mySlider) {
picno=5;
}
with (mySlider2) {
picno=5;
}
}
```

STEP 3: INSERT THE LARGE IMAGES

Here you insert the large filmstrip, add a mask, and add some ActionScript.

■ Insert a new layer, *bigfilmstrip.* Drag in your large images and line them up side by side.

■ Select all the images and choose **Insert** ➢ **Convert to Symbol**. Make it a movie clip and call it *filmstrip big.* Line it up so that the left edge is at x=0 (the left edge of the Stage). If necessary, use a **200%** or **400%** zoom and line it up manually.

■ With the symbol selected, type *mySlider* in the **Instance Name** text box of the **Property inspector.**

■ Add a new layer and name it *mask.* On *mask,* draw a filled rectangle with no stroke the size of one image. Place it over the leftmost image. **Right-click** (Win)/**Ctrl-click** (Mac) the *mask* layer and choose **Mask** from the menu.

■ Click *filmstrip big* and open or expand the **Actions** panel. Type or paste in the following ActionScript. (You can find this by clicking *filmstrip big* in **25.fla**, which is in the Techniques folder of the CD-ROM.)

```
onClipEvent(load) {
//change picno
//and totalpics
//to a different number
//if you have more or
//less than 5 images
picno=5;
totalpics=5;
}
onClipEvent (enterFrame) {
//the picture number times the
//width of the pictures

//minus one half the width of the
//pictures
newdist =
(((picno*(_width/totalpics)-
(.5*_width) - _x)) / 3);
_x = _x+newdist;

}
```

STEP 4: ADD THE MOTION BLUR

You add a layer for the motion blur and add some ActionScript to control the movement.

- Select Frame 1 of the *bigfilmstrip* layer. Choose **Edit ➢ Copy Frames**.
- Insert a new layer, call it *motionblur,* and drag it below *bigfilmstrip*. Choose **Edit ➢ Paste Frames**.
- Select the *filmstrip big* symbol. In the **Property inspector**, type *mySlider2* in the **Instance Name** text box.

NOTE

If you have difficulty being able to see all your images in the work area, you may want to create one large JPEG image in an image editor and import that.

- With *filmstrip big* selected, open or expand the **Actions** panel. Type or paste the following ActionScript. It is the same as the ActionScript for the *mySlider* instance, but the **newdist** line uses a **4** to define a slower speed (instead of a **3**).

```
onClipEvent(load) {
picno=5;
totalpics=5;
//change picno
//and totalpics
//to a different number
//if you have more or
//less than 5 images
}
onClipEvent (enterFrame) {
//the picture number times the width
//of the pictures
//minus one half the width of the
//pictures
newdist =
(((picno*(_width/totalpics)-
(.5*_width) - _x)) / 4);
_x = _x+newdist;
}
```

- Select the *mySlider* instance of *big filmstrip* on the *bigfilmstrip* layer. In the Property inspector, choose **Alpha** from the drop-down list and set the alpha to **50**.
- Drag the buttons layer beneath **Layer 1** to hide the buttons.
- Test your movie and click the buttons to see the images scroll with motion blur.

PAN AND ZOOM AN IMAGE

24.1 (CP 15)

Y ou can let your viewers pan an image in any direction (scroll the view horizontally), or zoom in or out, so they can see an image more clearly or decide which part of it they want to focus on.

STEP 1: IMPORT AN IMAGE

First, import or draw an image and convert it to a movie clip symbol.

- Start with a new movie. Change the name of **Layer 1** to *my picture*. Import a wide image (**File** ➢ **Import**). You can also draw a wide scene, although this technique is more impressive with a photo or other bitmap scene.
- To center the image, cut and paste it or use the **Align** panel (**Window** ➢ **Align**).

> **NOTE**
>
> Look for **24.fla** in the Techniques folder of the CD-ROM for our example of a panning/zooming interactive movie.

- Choose **Insert** ➢ **Convert to Symbol**. Make it a movie clip and name it *myPic*.
- Open the Property inspector (**Window** ➢ **Properties**) and click the **Expand/Collapse** arrow to expand it. In the **Instance Name** text box, type *myPic* to give it an instance name.

STEP 2: MAKE A BUTTON

You need to make two buttons for users to click when they zoom in and out.

- Choose **Insert** ➢ **New Symbol**. Make it a button and name it *zoom*.
- Draw a button. Make the **Up** and **Over** frames the same, but change the button image for the **Down** frame, so users see the difference when they click.
- Click **Scene 1** to return to the main Timeline.
- Add a new layer and name it *buttons*.
- Click the **Eye** column of the *my picture* layer to hide your scene.
- Drag two instances of *zoom* onto the *buttons* layer. Place them at the bottom two corners of the Stage.

STEP 3: CREATE A MASK

You need to create a mask around the Stage to hide parts of the picture that are to the left or to the right.

- Insert a new layer below the *buttons* layer and name it *mask*.

> **TIP**
>
> You can paste the ActionScript in from Frame 1 of the *actions* layer of **24.fla**.

- Draw a rectangle with a colored fill and no stroke that matches the size of the **Stage**. Choose **Insert** ➢ **New Symbol**. Make it a movie clip and name it *myMask*. Give it an instance name, *thisMask*.
- **Right-click** (Win)/**Ctrl-click** (Mac) the *mask* layer and choose **Mask** from the menu to make the layer a mask.

STEP 4: ADD THE ACTIONSCRIPT FOR THE FRAMES

Now you add ActionScript to control the movie.

- Add a new layer and name it *actions*.
- Click Frame 1. Open (**Window** ➢ **Actions**) or expand the **Actions** panel.
- Click the **View Control** button and choose **Expert** mode.
- Type or paste the following ActionScript. This ActionScript sets up the initial conditions for the size of the movie.

```
//initialize the variables
//newX is the x variable which moves
//the picture sideways.

//newY is the y variable which
//Moves the picture up and down.

//newScale keeps track of the
//scale of the picture

    newX=_root.myPic._x;
    newY=_root.myPic._y;
```

```
    newScale=100;
    initial_imageWidth=myPic._width;
    imageWidth=initial_imageWidth;

initial_imageHeight=myPic._height;
    imageHeight=initial_imageHeight;
```

■ Add a keyframe (**F6**) in Frame 2 of the *actions* layer. Type or paste the following ActionScript, which determines how the image appears, depending on where the mouse cursor is located:

```
//If the mouse is on the first ten
//pixels of the mask or less,
//then set the x position of myPic to
//four pixels more than what it
//previously was, but only if the
//previous X position is less than or
//equal to half of the imagewidth
//which is set by frame 1 or the zoom
//buttons.

if (_xmouse<=10){
    if(newX <= (imageWidth/2)){
        newX=newX+4;
        myPic._x =newX;
    }
}
//If the mouse is on the top ten
//pixels of the mask, or higher
//then set the y position of myPic to
//four pixels more then what it
//previously was, but only if the
//previous y position is less than or
//equal to half of the imageHeight
//which is set by frame 1 or the zoom
//buttons.

if (_ymouse<=10){
    if(newY <= (imageHeight/2)){
```

```
        newY=newY+4;
        myPic._y=newY;
    }
}
//If the mouse is on the last ten
//pixels of the mask or more, from
//the right,
//then set the x position of myPic to
//four pixels less than what it
//previously was, but only if myPic
//will still be almost completely
//under the mask.

if (_xmouse>=(thisMask._width-10)) {
    if(newX >= (imageWidth/2)-
(imageWidth-thisMask._width)){
    newX=newX-4;
    myPic._x=newX;
}
}
//If the mouse is on the bottom ten
//pixels of the mask, or lower
//then set the y position of myPic to
//four pixels less than what it
//previously was, but only if the
//myPic will still be almost
//completely under the mask.
if (_ymouse>=(thisMask._height-10)) {
    if(newY >= (imageHeight/2)-
(imageHeight-thisMask._height)){
    newY=newY-4;
    myPic._y=newY;
}
}
```

■ Add a keyframe (**F6**) in Frame 3 of the *actions* layer. Type or paste the following ActionScript:

```
gotoAndPlay(2);
```

- Close or collapse the **Actions** panel.
- Select the Frames 3s on all the layers and insert a frame (**F5**).

STEP 5: ADD THE ACTIONSCRIPT FOR THE BUTTONS

Now you program the buttons to zoom in and out.

- Select the left button to zoom out (make the scene smaller). Open the **Actions** panel and type or paste in the following ActionScript:

```
on (press) {
newscale=newscale-10;
imagewidth=initial_imagewidth*
(newscale/100);

imageheight=initial_imageheight*
newscale/100);

_root.myPic._xscale=newscale;
_root.myPic._yscale=newscale;
}
```

- Select the right button to zoom in (make the scene bigger). Type or paste in the following ActionScript:

```
on (press) {
newscale=newscale+10;
imagewidth=initial_imagewidth*
(newscale/100);

imageheight=initial_imageheight*
(newscale/100);

_root.myPic._xscale=newscale;
_root.myPic._yscale=newscale;
}
```

Test your movie. Move the cursor around to pan the image. Click the left button to zoom out and the right button to zoom in.

> **NOTE**
>
> You may want to add instructions for your viewers, such as labels on the buttons and some text, explaining that they should move the cursor around to pan across the scene.

MAKE A SCROLLING VIRTUAL REALITY PANORAMA

25.1

I n this technique, you drag to the left or right to see 360 degrees of a panoramic view.

STEP 1: IMPORT A PANORAMIC IMAGE

First you import your panoramic image.

- Start with a new movie. Choose **File** ➢ **Import** to import an appropriate image that can be used for a panorama. It needs to have some overlap where the image is repeated. We created our image in Corel's Bryce, a program that makes landscapes.
- Choose **Modify** ➢ **Break Apart** to break apart the image.

- Choose **Insert** ➢ **Convert to Symbol**. Save it as a movie clip and name it *pic360*.
- Delete *pic360* from the Stage. (It's in the **Library**.)

STEP 2: PLACE AND TWEEN THE IMAGE

You insert the image and motion tween it to move across the Stage.

- Insert a new layer, *Layer 2*.
- Drag *pic360* from the **Library** and place it at the right edge of the **Stage**.
- Insert a keyframe (**F6**) at Frame 300 of *Layer 2*. Insert a frame (**F5**) at Frame 300 of *Layer 1*.
- Select Frames 1 through 300 and choose **Motion** from the **Tween** drop-down list of the **Property inspector**.
- Click Frame 1 and press **Shift** as you drag *pic360* so that it is flush with the left edge of the **Stage**. (Pressing **Shift** ensures that the image moves horizontally.)
- Drag the red playhead until you find two frames that are identical (the picture is centered the same way over the **Stage**). Insert keyframes (**F6**) at these points. Select the frames after the highest keyframe and choose **Remove Frames**. Select the frames before the lowest keyframe and remove frames again. Doing this ensures that the movie starts and ends in the same place.
- Test the movie to make sure that the scene goes "around" one time. Note the total number of frames. You'll need this number later.

STEP 3: CONVERT THE ANIMATION TO A MOVIE CLIP

Convert the animation to a movie clip and drag it onto the main Timeline.

- Select both layers and choose **Edit** ➢ **Cut Frames**.
- Choose **Insert** ➢ **New Symbol**. Make a movie clip named *my360mc*.
- Click Frame 1 and choose **Edit** ➢ **Paste Frames**.
- Click **Scene 1** to return to the main **Timeline**.
- Insert a new layer. Name it *movingleft*. Delete the other two layers. Remove all frames except Frame 1 by selecting them and **right-clicking** (Win)/**Ctrl-clicking** (Mac) and choosing **Remove Frames**.
- Drag *my360mc* onto Frame 1. Center the frame over the Stage.
- With the movie clip selected, open (**Window** ➢ **Actions**) or expand the **Actions** panel. Type or paste in the following ActionScript. You can find this ActionScript by opening **25.fla**, selecting the symbol, and opening the Actions panel.

```
onClipEvent(load){
countframe=1;
//enter the number of frames in the
//movieclip in lastframe.
lastframe=170;
}


onClipEvent(enterFrame) {
//if the cursor is on the far right
//of the screen,

//play the movie backward
if (_root._xmouse>=450) {
countframe=countframe-1;
if (countframe<=0) {
countframe=lastframe;
        }
gotoAndPlay(countframe);
```

```
    }
//if the cursor is in the middle of
//the screen,
//stop the movie
if (_root._xmouse<=450 &&
_root._xmouse>=100) {
stop();
    }
//if the cursor is on the far left of
//the screen,
//play the movie forwards
if (_root._xmouse<=100) {
countframe=countframe+1;
if (countframe>=lastframe + 1) {
countframe=0;
        }
gotoAndPlay(countframe);
    }
}
```

STEP 4: CREATE A MASK

You need to create a mask to hide the part of the panorama that's off the Stage.

- Insert a new layer and name it *mask.*
- On Frame 1 of *mask,* draw a rectangle with a colored fill and no stroke. Make it the exact size of the Stage. (The default is 550 x 400 pixels. You can check the size of your **Stage** by choosing **Modify ➢ Document.**) Use the **Property inspector's** (**Window ➢ Properties**) **H** and **W** text boxes to set the size exactly. (Expand the **Property inspector** if necessary.)
- **Right-click** (Win)/**Ctrl-click** (Mac) and choose **Mask.**

Test the movie. Move the cursor to the right to move the scene to the right and vice versa. When you place the cursor in the center of the Stage, the movie stops.

NOTE

In line 4, change the *lastframe* value to the number of frames in the movieclip. The numbers 450 and 100 in the ActionScript determine at which x location the movie plays forward, stops, and plays back. If you have a different size Stage from the default 550 x 400 Stage size, you may want to change these numbers.

DRAGGABLE MASK

26.1

A mask displays what is inside a shape, hiding everything outside of the shape. A draggable mask lets viewers drag the shape to choose what they want to display. Who knows what surprises will be revealed?

STEP 1: CREATE THE BACKGROUND

Start with a new movie. Change the layer name to *background*. Draw or import the background that the draggable mask will reveal.

STEP 2: CREATE A MOVIE CLIP

To make the mask draggable, you need a button inside a movie clip. To create an empty movie clip, choose **Insert** ➢ **New Symbol**, make it a movie clip, and name it *maskmovie*. Click **Scene 1** to return to the main **Timeline**.

> **NOTE**
>
> Look for our draggable mask in **26.fla** in the Techniques folder of the CD-ROM.

STEP 3: CREATE A BUTTON

Now you create the button that will go inside the movie clip.

- Choose **Insert** ➢ **New Symbol**, make it a button, and name it *maskbutton.*
- In the **Up** frame, draw a shape for your mask. Fill it with a solid color. (You can leave the rest of the button frames blank.)
- Click **Scene 1** to return to the main **Timeline.**

STEP 4: MAKE THE MOVIE CLIP DRAGGABLE

To make the movie clip draggable, you need a button inside the movie clip.

- Open the **Library** (**Window** ➢ **Library**) and double-click *maskmovie* to edit it. Drag an instance of *maskbutton* onto the Stage.
- With *maskbutton* selected, open the **Actions** panel (**Window** ➢ **Actions**).
- In the menu on the left, click **Actions** ➢ **Movie Clip Control** and double-click **startDrag.** Select the top line of ActionScript. In the top area of the panel, uncheck **Release** and check **Press** so that the dragging starts when you press the mouse button.

- Click the last line of code and double-click **stopDrag** from the **Movie Clip Control** menu. Your code should now look like this:

```
on(press){
    startDrag("");
on(release)
}
    stopDrag();
```

- Close or hide the **Actions** panel.
- Click **Scene 1** to return to the main Timeline.

STEP 5: SET UP THE MASK

Create the mask.

- Add a new layer and name it *mask.* Drag an instance of *maskmovie* onto Frame 1 of the *mask* layer.
- **Right-click** (Win)/**Ctrl-click** (Mac) the *mask* layer and choose **Mask** from the menu.

Test the movie and drag the mask around to reveal what is underneath!

> **TIP**
>
> Although it's not necessary, you can convert an imported image to a symbol. Choose Insert ➢ Convert to symbol, make it a graphic symbol, and name it *background.*

INTERACTIVE SHADOWS

27.1 (CP 17)

The viewer moves a cursor that acts as a virtual light. Shadows on other objects move, reflecting the changing position of the light.

STEP 1: CREATE THE TEXT

Create the text for the shadow and then the text's shadow.

- Type some text in any color except gray. Choose **Insert** ➢ **Convert to Symbol**. Name the symbol *myText*, make it a movie clip, and click **OK**.
- Delete the text (it's in the Library) and use the same text settings to type the same text again. This time make the color a light gray. Choose **Insert** ➢ **Convert to Symbol**. Name the symbol *shadow*, make it a movie clip, and click **OK**.

NOTE

Watch our shadows move in **27.fla** in the Techniques folder of the CD-ROM.

- With the symbol still selected, type *shadow* in the **Instance Name** text box of the Property inspector. This instance name will be used in the ActionScript.
- Delete the text (it's in the Library).

STEP 2: CREATE THE CURSOR

You create a draggable cursor that represents a light.

- Draw an image to represent a light. We drew a sun.
- Select the sun and choose **Insert** ➢ **Convert to Symbol**. Make it a movie clip and call it *sun*. Click **OK**.
- With the sun still selected, type *sun* in the **Instance Name** text box of the **Property inspector**. This instance name will be used in the ActionScript.

TIP

Here's how we created our sun. Draw a circle with no stroke. Open the Color Mixer (**Window** ➢ **Color Mixer**) and chose Radial from the Fill Style drop-down list. Make the leftmost marker a yellow-orange color. Click in the middle to add a new marker and make it white. Make the rightmost marker white with an alpha of 0.

NOTE

Go to **27.fla**, select the sun, and open the Action panel. You can copy the ActionScript from there and paste it into the Action panel of your movie. The first four lines make your sun a draggable cursor. The rest position the x and y coordinates of *shadow* according to the location of *sun*.

STEP 3: ADD THE ACTIONSCRIPT

You add ActionScript to make the sun a draggable cursor and to specify how the *shadow* movie clip moves in relation to *myText* and *sun*.

- With the sun still selected, open the **Actions** panel (**Window** ➢ **Actions**). Click the **View Options** button and choose **Expert** mode. Type the following in the ActionScript panel:

```
onClipEvent (load) {
Mouse.hide();
startDrag("", true);
}
onClipEvent (enterFrame) {
_root.shadow._y = (((_root.myText._y-
_root.sun._y)*.05)+_root.myText._y);
_root.shadow._x = (((_root.myText._x-
_root.sun._x)*.05)+_root.myText._x);
}
```

- Close or hide the **Action** panel.

STEP 4: PLACE THE SYMBOLS ON THE STAGE

Here you position the text and the cursor.

- Change the name of the current layer to *sun*. With the *sun* movie clip selected, type *sun* in the

Instance Name text box of the Property inspector. This instance name is used in the Action Script.

■ Add a new layer and name it *shadow.* Drag *shadow* from the **Library** (**Window ➤ Library**) onto the **Stage**. Cut and paste it to center it. Type *shadow* in the **Instance Name** text box of the **Property inspector**. This instance name is used in the Action Script.

■ Add a new layer and name it *myText.* Drag *myText* from the Library onto the Stage. Cut and paste the layer to center it. Type *myText* in the **Instance Name** text box of the **Property inspector**. This instance name is used in the Action Script.

■ Drag the layer, *sun,* to the top of the layer listing. You now have three layers, with *sun* on top, followed by *myText,* and then *shadow* at the bottom.

Test the movie to see the results. As you move your mouse, the sun follows, and the shadow moves in the opposite direction.

REMINDER

You can use the Align panel (Window ➤ Align) to place both symbols exactly on top of each other.

CHAPTER 6

USER INTERFACES

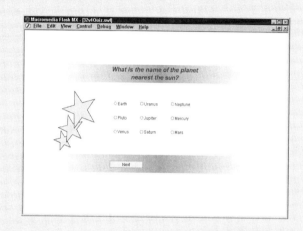

Flash is ideally suited to creating entire Web sites. Aside from animation, you can create complex user interfaces — buttons, scroll bars, checkboxes, menus, tabs, forms, and more. You can also create cursors and mouse trails, just for fun. In this chapter, we describe 15 user interface techniques.

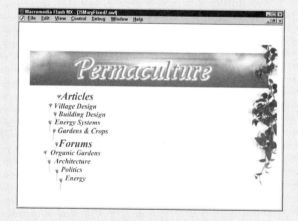

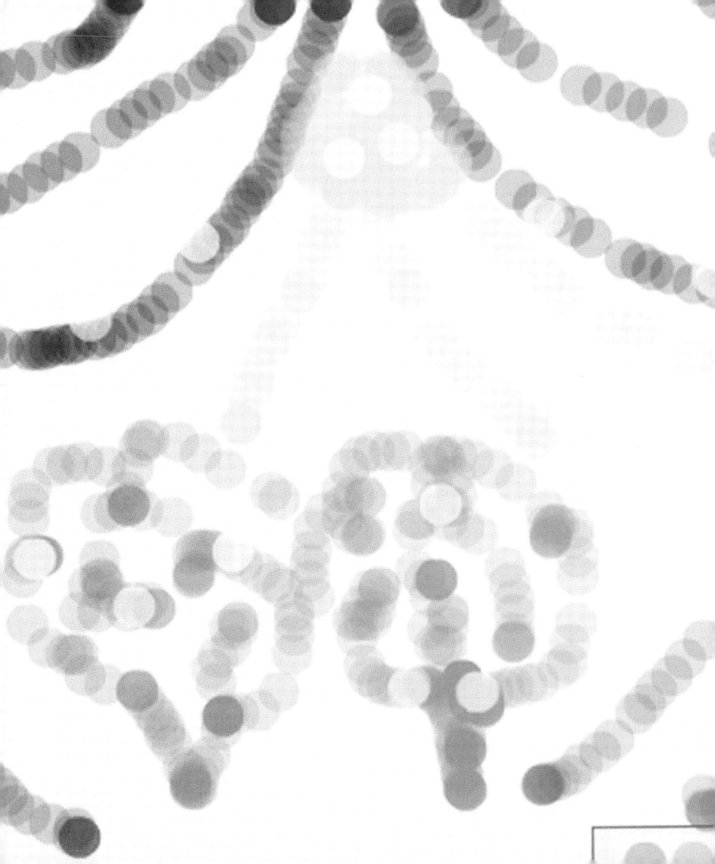

MOUSE TRAILS

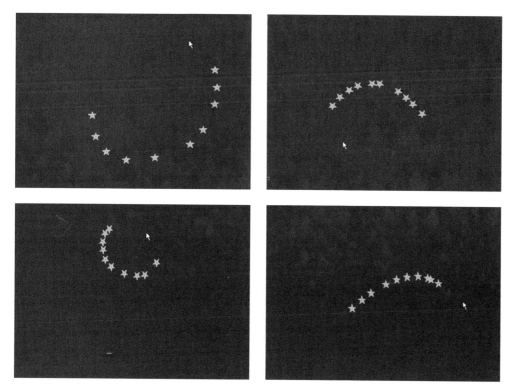

28.1 (CP 18)

M ouse trails are graphics that follow the mouse. Wherever the mouse goes, they go, too. Mouse trails are lots of fun, easy to create, and very flashy.

STEP 1: CREATE THE TRAILING GRAPHIC

Create the graphic that you want to follow the mouse.

- Choose **Insert** ➢ **New Symbol**. Make it a movie clip and name it *trails*.
- Draw any small graphic that you want. It shouldn't be much larger than the mouse arrow. Click **Scene 1** to return to the main **Timeline**.
- Change the layer name to *trails*. Open the **Library** (**Window** ➢ **Library**) and drag an instance of *trails* onto the **Stage**. Cut and paste the layer to center it (or use the **Align** panel). With the symbol still selected,

type *trail 1* in the **Instance Name** text box of the
Property inspector (**Window** ➢ **Properties**).

- Click the symbol. Copy and paste the symbol to
make a copy on top of the original. Give it an
instance name of *trail 2*. Continue to make copies,
named sequentially, until you have as many as you
want. (We used **10**.)

STEP 2: CREATE A BACKGROUND

Insert a layer named *background,* and add any background you want. Drag it below the *trails* layer.

STEP 3: ADD ACTIONSCRIPT

Add ActionScript to track the position of the cursor.

- Insert a new layer and name it *actions*.
- In Frame 1, type or paste in the following
ActionScript. You can find it in Frame 1 of **28.fla**,
which is on the CD-ROM.

```
//Enter the number of trails below.
numberOfTrails=10;
//Create two new arrays. One will
//store the
//X positions of the mouse and the
//other will
//hold the Y positions of the mouse.
pastMouseXPosition=new Array;
pastMouseYPosition=new Array;
//Load the first six values of each
//array with
```

> **NOTE**
>
> Find our stars trailing your mouse in **28.fla** in
> the Techniques folder of the CD-ROM.

```
//the current mouse position.
for (i=1;i<=numberOfTrails;i++) {
    pastMouseXPosition[i]=_xmouse;
    pastMouseYPosition[i]=_ymouse;
}
countframe=numberOfTrails;
```

- Insert a keyframe (**F6**) in Frame 2 of the *actions*
layer and type or paste in the following
ActionScript. You can find it in Frame 2 of **28.fla**,
which is on the CD-ROM.

```
//Put the mouse position into the
//past mouse position arrays.
pastMouseXPosition[countframe]
=_xmouse;
pastMouseYPosition[countframe]
=_ymouse;
//Set the x,y position of the mouse
//trails according to the
//previous x,y positions of the
//mouse.
for (i=1;i<=numberOfTrails;i++) {
setProperty("trail"+i,_x,
pastMouseXPosition[countframe-i-1]);
setProperty("trail"+i,_y,
pastMouseYPosition[countframe
-i-1]);
}
countframe=countframe+1;
//Don't let the array get too big.
//Start over after 1000 frames
if (countframe>=999){
    gotoAndPlay(1);
}
```

- Insert a keyframe in Frame 3 and type or paste
it in:

```
gotoAndPlay(2);
```

- Add a frame (**F5**) in Frame 3 of the *trails* and *background* layers.

Test the movie and move your mouse furiously about. Try as you might, you can't shake those trailing symbols.

REMINDER

Be sure to enter the number of symbols you placed on the Stage in the second line of code. We used 10, but you need to adjust this if you used a different number of symbols.

TABBED MENU

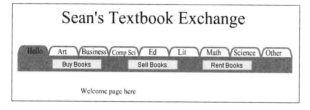

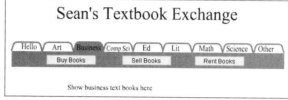

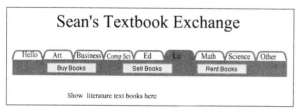

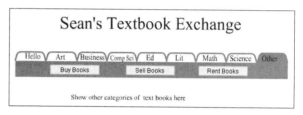

29.1

These tabs are similar to the tabbed menu at the top of Amazon.com. Clicking a tab brings the user to another frame that displays the content of that frame.

STEP 1: CREATE THE LAYERS

In Step 1, you set up the layers and add a little ActionScript.

- Start with a new movie. Insert four new layers (**Insert ➢ Layer**), for a total of five. Starting from the top layer, name them *actions*, *labels*, *tabs*, *bar*, and *content*.
- Click Frame 1 of the *actions* layer. Open (**Window ➢ Actions**) or expand the **Actions** panel. Click the **View Control** button and choose **Normal** mode. Choose **Actions ➢ Movie Control** and double-click **Stop**. Close or collapse the **Actions** panel.

NOTE

Look for our tabbed menu in the Techniques folder of the CD-ROM in **29.fla**.

STEP 2: CREATE THE BAR

As you can see in **Figure 29.1**, the tabs grow out of a bar. The bar may also contain buttons.

Use the **Rectangle** tool to create the bar on the *bar layer*, running across the entire **Stage**. If you want, add buttons. Lock the layer.

STEP 3: CREATE THE TABS

Create the tabs and add some ActionScript.

- On the *tabs* layer, draw a tab. The fill should contrast with the color of the bar, and the bottom should be flat so that it seems to be attached to the bar. Move the tab to meet the top of the bar, as shown in **Figure 29.1**.
- With the tab selected, choose **Insert** ➢ **Convert to Symbol**. Make it a button and call it *tab*.

WIDTH OF THE TAB

To calculate the width of the tab, divide the width of the bar by the number of tabs you need. Our tabs were made by drawing a rounded rectangle with an arc of 10 pixels. The fill contrasts with the bar, but the stroke matches it. Then we used the new Flash MX tapering feature. Select the tab, click the Free Transform tool, press Ctrl+Shift (Win)/⌘+Shift (Mac), and drag out on one of the outside bottom corners until you get an angle you like. Then draw a horizontal line just above the bottom rounded corners and delete the lower segmented sections to get a flat bottom.

- Copy the tab to the **Clipboard** and paste it back in. Drag the copy next to the first tab. Continue to paste in new tabs until you have all the tabs you need.
- Select the leftmost tab. Open or display the **Actions** panel. Using **Normal** mode, choose **Actions** ➢ **Movie Control**. Double-click **GoTo**. At the top of the **Actions** panel, click **Go to and Stop**, as shown in **Figure 29.2**. Click the first line of ActionScript. At the top of the panel, uncheck **Release** and check **Press**.
- Select the second tab from the left. Add the same ActionScript as you did for the leftmost tab, but change the frame number to 2. Do the same with the rest of the tabs, making sure that each one says **GoTo and Stop** (**GoTo and Play** is the default) and each points to the next frame.
- On the *tabs* layer, insert a keyframe (**F6**) for each tab. For example, if you have five tabs, you should have a keyframe in Frames 1 through 5.

STEP 4: CREATE THE CHOSEN TAB

An important characteristic of tabbed menus is that when you choose a tab, it changes color to match the color of the bar.

- Open the **Library** (**Window** ➢ **Library**) and drag a copy of *tab* onto the Stage. Choose **Modify** ➢ **Break Apart**. Use the **Paint Bucket** tool to fill the tab with the color of the bar.
- Select the tab. Choose **Insert** ➢ **Convert to Symbol**. Make it a button and call it *chosentab*.
- Click Frame 1. Delete the leftmost tab. Move *chosentab* in its place. Use the **Align** panel to align the tabs if necessary.
- Click Frame 2. Delete the second-from-left tab. From the **Library**, drag a copy of *chosentab* to replace the deleted tab. Continue this process for all the tabs.

STEP 5: EXTEND THE OTHER LAYERS

You now need to add frames and keyframes to extend the other layers.

- Unlock the *bar* layer. Click the frame that corresponds to the number of tabs you have. Choose **Insert ➢ Frame**.
- Click the same number frame on the *actions* layer and insert a frame.
- On the *content* layer, add a keyframe for each frame containing a tab.

STEP 6: ADD LABELS

Lock the *tabs* layer. On Frame 1 of the *labels* layer, add labels for each tab. Click the frame corresponding to the number of tabs you have and choose **Insert ➢ Frame**.

STEP 7: ADD CONTENT

Each frame contains different content. For each frame, create the content you want to show when that frame's tab is clicked.

Test your movie and click the tabs. Watch the content change.

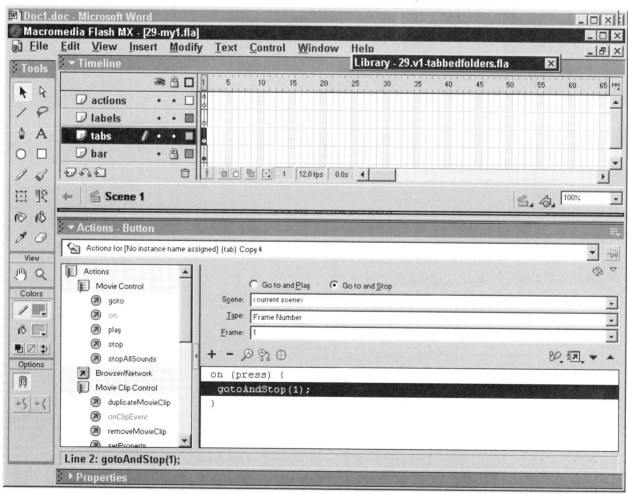

29.2

SCROLL BARS

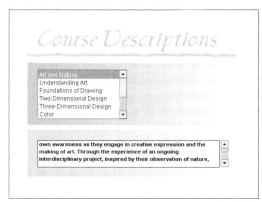
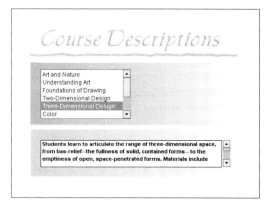

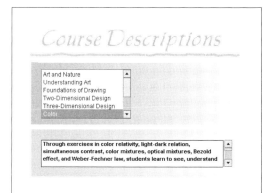
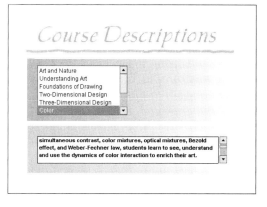

30.1 (CP 20)

*S*croll bars are one of several user interface items that you can add to a site. Users scroll through as they read the text. Use scrolling text when you don't have enough room on a Web page for all the text you need to display.

STEP 1: INSERT A COMBOBOX

You insert a **ComboBox** component and create its labels and data.

- Start with a new movie. Add two new layers to the existing layer and name the three layers *actions*, *text*, and *background*.
- Click Frame 1 of the *text* layer. From the **Components** panel (**Window ➢ Components**), drag a **ComboBox** onto the **Stage**. (If the ComboBox is not wide enough, use the **Free Transform** tool to widen it.)

■ With the **ComboBox** selected, open (**Window** ➢ **Properties**) or expand the **Property inspector**. Click the *Labels* row and then the **Magnifying Glass** button to the right of the row to display the **Values** dialog box, shown in **Figure 30.2**. Use this dialog box to create the list that will display in the **ComboBox**.

■ Click the plus sign to add an item. Type the item in the **Value** column. Continue to add items. When you are done, click **OK**.

■ Click the **Data** row then the **Magnifying Glass** button to the right of the row to display the same **Values** dialog box, shown in **Figure 30.2**.

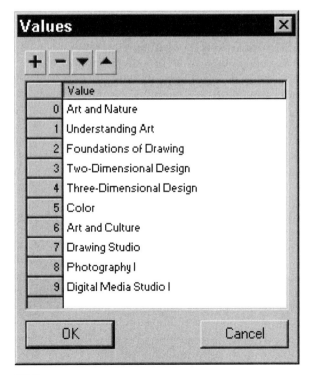

30.2

However, this time, you are specifying data that will be used in the ActionScript but not displayed. Enter values for each item, starting with **i1** and continuing for each item you want to list. Our example has ten items, so we used **i1** through **i10**.

■ In the **Property inspector**, enter **PickItem** for the **Change Handler**.

■ In the **Property inspector's Instance Name** text box, type *myList*.

STEP 2: CREATE A SCROLLING DYNAMIC TEXT BOX

You create the scrolling text box that gets its data from the ActionScript. You could also get the data from an outside source, such as a separate text file.

■ Create a text box. In the **Property inspector**, choose **Dynamic Text** from the **Property inspector's Text Type** drop-down list. Give it an instance name of *description* and a variable name of *itemDescription*. Click the **Show Border Around Text** button to turn on the border and click the **Selectable** button to turn off selectability (which is on by default). From the **Line Type** drop-down box, choose **Multiline**. Text should be left-justified.

■ From the **Components** panel, drag a **ScrollBar** onto the text box. It should attach to the right side of the text box and resize automatically.

■ Type some dummy text in the box. You need to be sure to type enough text, longer than any of the text you want to appear in the text box, to activate the scrolling feature. So start writing your first novel here.

■ Insert a frame (**F5**) in Frame 2.

STEP 3: ADD THE BACKGROUND

On the *background* layer (which should be the bottom layer), add whatever background you want. Insert a frame (**F5**) in Frame 2.

STEP 4: ADD THE ACTIONSCRIPT

You add the ActionScript that displays the appropriate course description for the course selected in the ComboBox.

■ Click Frame 1 of the *actions* layer. Open (**Window ➢ Actions**) or expand the **Actions** panel and type or paste (from Frame 1 of the *actions* layer of **30.fla**) the following ActionScript:

```
//Blank out the dummy data in the
//dynamic text box. It was necessary to
//put it in so that the scroll bar
//recognized that it needed to be
//able to scroll.
itemDescription="";
```

■ Insert a keyframe (**F6**) in Frame 2 of the *actions* layer. Type or paste (from Frame 2 of the *actions* layer of **30.fla**) the following ActionScript.

```
stop();
//PickItem is called by the combo box.
function PickItem() {
//Get the value from the combo box
//and put it into the variable "myVar".
    myVar=myList.getValue();
//set the dynamic text box to the
//appropriate course description.
    if (myVar=="i1"){
    itemDescription="Students gain
an appreciation for the mechanics
of creation as experienced in the
natural world and within the realm
of one's own awareness as they engage
in creative expression and the making
of art. Through the experience of an
ongoing interdisciplinary project,
```

```
inspired by their observation of
nature, students prepare for a unique
aesthetic presentation.";
    }
    if (myVar=="i2"){
    itemDescription="Expressions of
art are a celebration of life. These
courses culture a deep appreciation—
even a sense of awe—for all art forms.
This survey of the arts features
lectures, seminars, and research into
the greatest painters, poets, and
composers, whose works continue to
inspire the public and stir the
creativity of all aspiring artists.";
    }
    if (myVar=="i3"){
    itemDescription="This course
introduces the fundamentals of
drawing, which includes observation
and organization of line, shape, and
tone in the compositional structure.";
    }
    if (myVar=="i4"){
    itemDescription="This creative
exploration in two-dimensional media
includes possibilities such as
drawing, painting, and collage. The
course culminates in the creation of
an artist's book.";
    }
    if (myVar=="i5"){
    itemDescription="Students learn
to articulate the range of three-
dimensional space, from bas-relief—
the fullness of solid, contained
forms— to the emptiness of open,
space-penetrated forms. Materials
include wood, paper, wire, plaster,
clay, and found objects.";
    }
    if (myVar=="i6"){
```

```
     itemDescription="Through
exercises in color relativity, light-
dark relation, simultaneous contrast,
color mixtures, optical mixtures,
Bezold effect, and Weber-Fechner law,
students learn to see, understand,
and use the dynamics of color
interaction to enrich their art.";
     }
     if (myVar=="i7"){
     itemDescription="Students
journey through the most inspiring
creations of human culture in art,
architecture, music, myth and film.
They examine how these works express
both unique cultural values and
universal values of consciousness.
This course focuses on the art and
culture of a particular region while
in residence abroad.";
     }
     if (myVar=="i8"){
     itemDescription="These courses
are dedicated to developing the
student's powers of observation and
imagination. Visual arts majors take
several drawing courses as they
advance through the curriculum.
Topics may include figure drawing,
still life drawing, drawing from
nature, and imaginative drawing. The
particular emphasis of each course is
specified by the instructor.";
```

```
     }
     if (myVar=="i9"){
     itemDescription="Students are
introduced to the black-and-white
world through the camera lens. They
learn basic camera techniques, black-
and-white film processing, and
darkroom procedures.";
     }
     if (myVar=="i10"){
     itemDescription="Students work
in the School's well-equipped color
computer lab on projects utilizing
computer art, animation, photography,
or video.";
}}
```

Test the movie and choose a course to see its description. Scroll down if necessary to see the entire description.

WARNING

You need to adjust this ActionScript by placing the descriptions you want in place of the descriptions in the ActionScript shown here, in each line after *itemDescription=*. Enclose your descriptions in quotation marks as shown in the ActionScript. Also, we used 10 descriptions; you need to adjust the number of descriptions for your own needs.

POP-UP WINDOWS

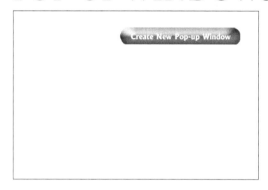 

 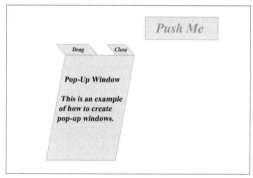

31.1
(Rose by Dale Divoky. Used with permission.)

A pop-up window appears when the viewer clicks a button. You can drag the window and close it. Here you see two versions.

STEP 1: CREATE THE POP-UP WINDOW

Create the artwork for the pop-up window.

■ Start with a new movie. Change the name of **Layer 1** to *popup window*. In Frame 1, draw the pop-up window. Include a title bar that users can use to drag the window around and a close button area for closing the window. See **Figure 31.1** for our examples.

■ Draw the artwork for a button that covers the area of your title bar. Select the artwork and choose **Insert ➤ Convert to Symbol**. Make it a button named *DragButton*. Add some text that identifies the window.

- Create a button that covers your Close button area. Add the text **Close**. Select the artwork and choose **Insert** ➢ **Convert to Symbol**. Make it a button named *CloseButton.*
- Select everything on the **Stage** and choose **Insert** ➢ **Convert to Symbol**. Make it a movie clip named *PopUp.*
- In the **Property inspector** (**Window** ➢ **Properties**), type *myPopUp1* in the **Instance Name** text box.

STEP 2: SET UP THE POP-UP WINDOW

You want the pop-up window in Frame 2 of its Timeline so that it doesn't appear when you first play the movie. It will appear only after you click a button. You also need to make the *DragButton* and *CloseButton* buttons work.

- Double-click **PopUp** to edit it. Click Frame 1 to select every item in the pop-up window.
- Press **Ctrl+X** (Win)/⌘+**X**(Mac) to cut the pop-up window to the **Clipboard**.
- Insert a keyframe (**F6**) in Frame 2.
- With Frame 2 selected, choose **Edit** ➢ **Paste in Place**.
- Click Frame 1. In the **Actions** panel (**Window** ➢ **Actions**), click the **View Options** button and choose **Normal** mode. From the **Actions** panel menu, choose **Actions** ➢ **Movie Control** and double-click **Stop**.
- Insert a keyframe in Frame 2. From the **Actions** panel menu, choose **Actions** ➢ **Movie Control** and double-click **Stop**.

- Select the *DragButton*. In the **Actions** panel, choose **Actions** ➢ **Movie Clip Control** and double-click **startDrag**. Select the first line of ActionScript that says **on** (**release**). Check the **Press** checkbox and uncheck the **Release** checkbox. Select the last line of ActionScript (the closing bracket) and double-click **stopDrag**. The ActionScript should read:

```
on (release) {
    startDrag("");
}
on (release) {
    stopDrag();
}
```

- Select the *CloseButton*. Double-click **GoTo** in the **Movie Control** section of the menu. The ActionScript should read:

```
on (release) {
    gotoAndPlay(1);
}
```

- Click **Scene 1** to return to the main **Timeline**. You should see the registration point of the pop-up window but nothing else.

STEP 3: ADD A BUTTON TO DISPLAY THE POP-UP WINDOW

Create a button that displays the pop-up window when you click it.

- Choose **Insert** ➢ **New Symbol**. Make it a button and call it *BringUpPopUp.*

- Draw any type of button you want.
- Click **Scene 1** to return to the main **Timeline**.
- Insert a new layer and name it *pushbutton.*
- Drag *BringUpPopUp* in from the **Library** into Frame 1 of the *pushbutton* layer. Select it and open or display the **Actions** panel. From the menu, choose **Actions** ➢ **Variables** and double-click **With**. With the **"with (<not set yet>)"** line of ActionScript selected, click the **Object** text box and then click the **Insert a Target Path** button to open the **Insert Target Path** dialog box, shown in **Figure 31.2**. Select *myPopUp1* and click **OK**.
- In the **Actions** ➢ **Movie Control** section of the menu, double-click Play. The ActionScript should look like the following:

```
on (release) {
    with (myPopUp1) {
        play();
    }
}
```

Test your movie and click the button to display the pop-up window.

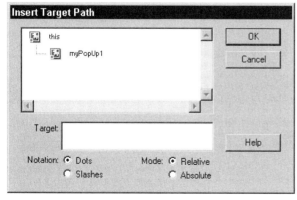

31.2

CREATE A MULTIPLE CHOICE QUIZ

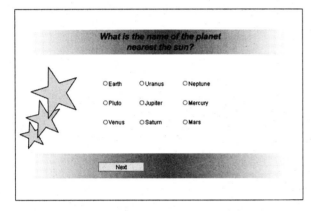

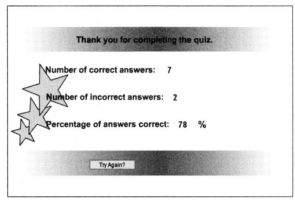

32.1 (CP 21)

A sk your viewers anything. Then grade them at the end of the quiz.

STEP 1: CREATE THE LAYERS

Start with a new movie. Add two new layers (**Insert** ➤ **Layer**). Rename the three layers *actions*, *radiobuttons*, and *Q&A*.

STEP 2: ADD RADIO BUTTONS FOR ANSWER CHOICES

In this step, you add radio buttons from Flash's collection of components. Quiz takers use these buttons to select an answer to the question.

NOTE

Take our quiz on the solar system in **32.fla,** which is in the Techniques folder of the CD-ROM.

■ In Frame 2 of the **radiobuttons** layer, insert a keyframe (**F6**). Open the **Components** panel (**Window ➤ Components**). Drag the radio button component onto the **Stage** as many times as you want. Place them and use the **Align** panel (**Window ➤ Align**) to line them up and distribute them evenly.

■ Open (**Window ➤ Properties**) or expand the **Property inspector**. Select the first radio button. You should see a list of parameters. Change the **Label** parameter to whatever you want the answer to read. (If you don't see the parameters, click the **Parameters** tab at the upper-right corner of the **Property inspector**.)

■ In the **Property inspector**, change the **Data** parameter to the answer. (In our example, **Data** and **Label** are the same. However, if you want to put letters or numbers before the answer, the **Data** parameter should only contain the answer, not the letter or number.) The **Property inspector** should look like **Figure 32.2.**

■ Select the other radio buttons in turn and change their **Label** and **Data** parameters.

WARNING

We experienced some trouble when working with components, such as computer crashing and screen freezing. We had to reboot many times. However, after the movie was set up, it worked fine. Save your work very often.

STEP 3: ADD THE QUESTION

Insert a keyframe in Frame 2 of the *Q&A* layer. Use the **Text** tool to add the question on the *Q&A* layer. Position the question and adjust the font and color to your liking.

STEP 4: ADD THE "NEXT" BUTTON

You add a button that is coded with the correct answer and also moves the quiz taker to the next question.

■ From the **Components** panel, drag a push button onto the **Stage** below the answers. Change its **Label** parameter in the **Property inspector** to **Next.** (You could also use **Submit** or something similar.) Change its **Click Handler parameter to** *yourAnswer.* This parameter is the name of a function that you define later in the ActionScript.

■ In the **Instance Name** text box of the **Property inspector**, type **Mercury** or the answer to the question. The instance name must match the **Data** parameter exactly.

■ Repeat Steps 2 through 4 for each question and set of answers. (In our example, the answers remain the same throughout (all nine planets), so we didn't add keyframes on the *radiobuttons* layer. You could do the same with a true/false quiz, where the available answers are always true and false.)

STEP 5: ADD A SCORING SCREEN

At the end of the quiz, you thank viewers for taking the quiz and show them their score.

■ Add a new keyframe after the last keyframe of the *Q&A* layer. Use the **Text** tool to add some text that says **Thank you for completing the quiz.**

■ Add three additional text blocks for correct and incorrect answers and the percentage. Also add a text box that contains only the % character. See **Figure 32.3.**

32.2

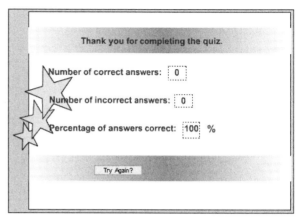

32.3

- Add a new text box to the right of the text box for correct answers. In the **Property inspector**, choose **Dynamic Text** from the **Text Type** drop-down list. In the **Var** text box of the **Property inspector**, type *rightAnswers*.
- Add a new text box to the right of the text box for incorrect answers. In the **Property inspector**, choose **Dynamic Text** from the **Text Type** drop-down list. In the **Var** text box of the **Property inspector**, type *wrongAnswers*.
- Add a new text box to the right of the text box for the percentage score. In the **Property inspector**, choose **Dynamic Text** from the **Text Type** drop-down list. In the **Var** text box of the **Property inspector**, type *yourGrade*.
- You should still have a **Next** button. Select this button and change its label in the **Property inspector** to **Try Again?** Set the **Click Handler** to *tryAgain*. Your screen should look like **Figure 32.3**.

STEP 6: ADD THE ACTIONSCRIPT

The ActionScript in Frame 1 resets the number of right and wrong answers to zero. The ActionScript in

> **TIP**
>
> In our example, we use the names of the planets. You could also use a letter number and an answer, A. 6 colors, for example.

Frame 2 creates the function used by the **Next** buttons to get the value of the radio button that was clicked, check if it's the right answer (by comparing it to the instance name), and count up the right and wrong answers.

- Click Frame 1 of the *actions* layer. Open (**Windows ➤ Actions**) or expand the **Actions** panel. Click the **View Mode** button and choose **Expert**. Type or paste in the following ActionScript. (You can find all the ActionScript in Frames 1 and 2 of **32.fla** in the Techniques folder of the CD-ROM.) This initializes the count of right and wrong answers.

```
answersRight=0;
answersWrong=0;
```

- Insert a keyframe in Frame 2 of the *actions* layer. Type or paste in the following ActionScript.

```
//Stop the movie at each frame
stop();
//This function is called by the next
//buttons
function yourAnswer(component) {
```

```
//Get the value of the radio
//button that has been pushed

thisAnswer=radioGroup.getValue();
//Get the instance name which is
//the correct answer
    rightAnswer=component._name;
//find out if the answer is
//Correct and tally the right or
//wrong answers
    if (rightAnswer == thisAnswer) {

rightAnswers=rightAnswers+1;
            } else {
    wrongAnswers=wrongAnswers+1;
    }
//Compute the grade percentage
    yourGrade=Math.round(100*
(rightanswers/
(rightanswers+wrongAnswers)))
//Go to the next frame
    gotoAndPlay(nextFrame());
    }
//This function is called when
//the tryAgain button is pushed
    function tryAgain() {
//Frame 1 initializes the
//tally of right and wrong answers to
//zero.
            gotoAndPlay(1);
    }
```

Test the movie and take the quiz!

USER RESPONSE FORM

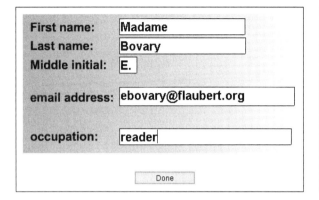

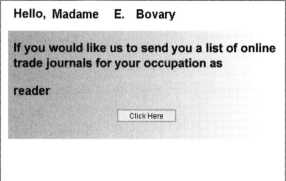

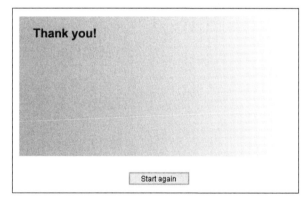

33.1

Create a form that collects information from viewers. In our example, we use this information elsewhere within the Flash file, but you can capture this information into a database or send it via e-mail by using a CGI script on the Web server. Contact your Web host for further information about using CGI scripts.

STEP 1: CREATE TEXT BOXES

Create text boxes for the static text (labels or instructions) and for the input text (that the users type in).

- Start with a new movie. Insert a new layer (**Insert ➢ Layer**). Rename the layers *text* and *actions*.
- In Frame 1 of the *text* layer, create text boxes that label the input you want to get. Common examples are **Name** and **Email address**. These

135

text boxes should all be static text, as displayed in the **Text Type** drop-down list of the **Property inspector** (**Windows** ➢ **Properties**).

■ Next to each text box, create a new text box. With the text box still selected, choose **Input Text** from the **Text Type** drop-down list of the **Property inspector**. Expand the **Property inspector** and click the **Show Border Around Text** button to create a border around the text box. Your screen should look something like the first screen in **Figure 33.1**.

STEP 2: ADD A BUTTON

Add a PushButton component to send the viewer to the next frame.

■ Open the **Components** panel (**Window** ➢ **Components**) and drag a **PushButton** onto the Stage. With the **PushButton** selected, change the label in the **Property inspector** to *Done* and the **Click Handler** to *EnteringComplete*. ActionScript in Frame 1 uses the *EnteringComplete* function.

STEP 3: CREATE THE SECOND FRAME

Create the second frame, which uses the input from the first frame.

■ Insert a new keyframe (**F6**) in Frame 2 of the *text* layer. You can see Frame 2 in the second screen of **Figure 33.1**. In this frame, you use the input from Frame 1. We just rearranged the existing input frames that contained the user's name, deleted the e-mail input frame, and added some new static text boxes.
■ Select the **PushButton**. Change its label to *Click Here* and its **Click Handler** to *OnClick*. *OnClick* is a function in the ActionScript of Frame 1.

STEP 4: CREATE THE THIRD FRAME

Create the third frame, which lets the user start from the beginning.

■ Insert a new keyframe (**F6**) in Frame 3 of the *text* layer. You can see Frame 3 in the third screen of **Figure 33.1**.
■ Add any static text boxes that you want.
■ Select the **PushButton** and change its label to **Start Again**. Change the **Click Handler** to *startAgain*. The *startAgain* function is used in the ActionScript.

STEP 5: ADD THE ACTIONSCRIPT

Add the ActionScript that creates the functions used by the three PushButtons.

■ Click Frame 1 of the *actions* layer. Type the following ActionScript or paste it in from Frame 1of the *actions* layer of **33.fla**.

```
InitializeData();
//calls the function below
stop();

//InitializeData blanks out all the
//input text.
function InitializeData() {
lastname="";
firstname="";
middleinitial="";
emailaddress="";
occupation="";
}
//EnteringComplete is called by the
//"Done" PushButton
//on Frame 1 of the text layer.
function EnteringComplete() {
    gotoAndStop(2);
}
```

```
//OnClick is called by the "Click
//Here" PushButton on
//Frame 2 of the text layer.
function OnClick(){
                    gotoAndStop(3);
}
//StartAgain is called by the "start
//again" PushButton on
//Frame 3 of the text layer.
function StartAgain(){
                    gotoAndStop(1);
}
```

■ Add a frame (**F5**) in Frame 3 of the *actions* layer.

Test the movie, fill out the form, and click the buttons to see how it works.

> **NOTE**
>
> See our input form in the Techniques folder of the CD-ROM in **33.fla**.

FORM VALIDATION

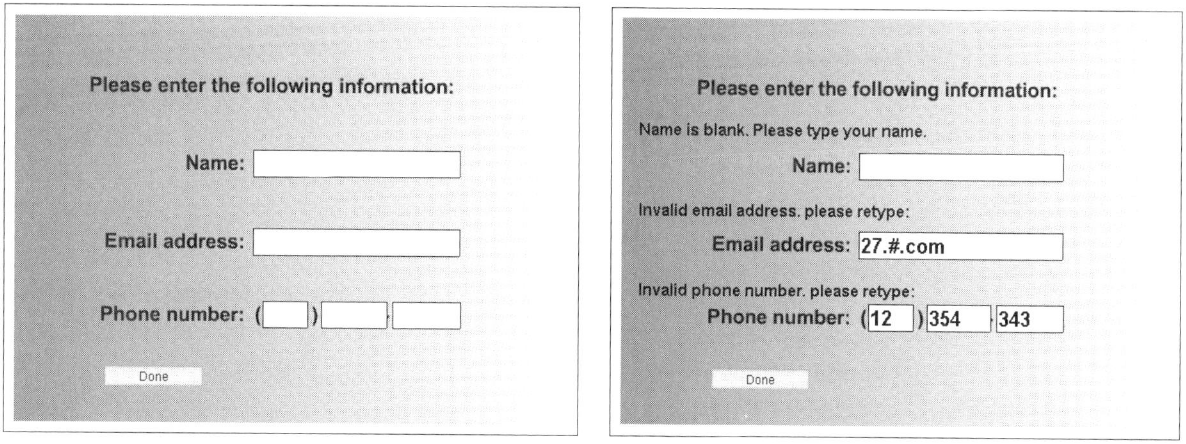

Please enter the following information:

Name:

Email address:

Phone number: ( ) -

Done

Please enter the following information:

Name is blank. Please type your name.

Name:

Invalid email address. please retype:

Email address: 27.#.com

Invalid phone number. please retype:

Phone number: (12)354 -343

Done

34.1

You should check that forms are correctly filled out. For example, you can check for missing data and incorrect e-mail addresses or phone numbers.

STEP 1: CREATE THE TEXT BOXES

Create the text boxes for the static, input, and dynamic text.

- Insert two layers. Name the three layers *actions*, *text*, and *background*.
- In Frame 1 of the *text* layer, create the static text boxes, as shown in **Figure 34.1**. The instructions (**Please enter the following information**, **Name:**, **Email address:**, and **Phone number:** are all static text (the default), so be sure that **Static Text** appears in the **Text Type** drop-down list of the **Property inspector** (**Windows** ➢ **Properties**).

■ Also in Frame 1, create the input text boxes. These are the blank boxes. Make sure that they are long enough for the information that users will type. For each input text box, select the box, choose **Input Text** from the **Text Type** drop-down list of the **Property inspector**, click the **Show Border Around Text** button (you may need to expand the **Property inspector**), and give it a variable name in the **Var** text box of the **Property inspector**. The phone number needs three input text boxes. The variable names are *name*, *emailAddress*, *areaCode*, *localExchange*, and *lastFourNumbers*.

■ Create text boxes for the error messages. They are dynamic text, so select each one, choose **Dynamic Text** from the **Text Type** drop-down list of the **Property inspector**, and give it a variable name. The variable names are *nameError*, *emailError*, and *phoneError*, respectively. Make sure that the Show Border Around Text is *not* active. The actual text of the errors messages is contained in the ActionScript, so you don't enter any text in these text boxes.

■ Use the **Align** panel (**Windows** ➢ **Align**) to line up and evenly distributed all the boxes.

STEP 2: INSERT A PUSHBUTTON

Place a **PushButton** for users to click when they finish entering data.

From the **Components** panel (**Window** ➢ **Components**), drag in a **PushButton**. In the **Property inspector**, change its **Label** to *Done* and its **Click Handler** to *EnteringComplete*. This function is used in the ActionScript.

STEP 3: CREATE THE NEXT SCREEN

Insert a keyframe (**F6**) in Frame 3 of the *text* layer. Delete all the text boxes and add a static text box with the text, **Thank you**.

Select the **PushButton**, change its label to **Start Again**, and change its **Click Handler** to *StartAgain*.

STEP 4: ADD THE ACTIONSCRIPT

Add the ActionScript that initializes the input boxes (sets them to empty) and uses the various functions to test for errors.

■ Insert a keyframe in Frame 2 of the *actions* layer. Open (**Window** ➢ **Actions**) or expand the **Actions** panel and type the following:

```
stop();
```

■ Insert a frame (**F5**) in Frame 3 of the *actions* layer.

■ Click Frame 1 of the *actions* layer and type or paste in (from Frame 1 of the *actions* layer of **34.fla** in the Techniques folder of the CD-ROM) the following ActionScript:

```
//Initialize the screen and get rid
//of all the previous info.
nameError="";
emailError="";
phoneError="";
name="";
emailaddress="";
areaCode="";
localExchange="";
lastFourNumbers="";
stop();

//This function is called by the
//button that the user clicks after
//entering data.
function EnteringComplete() {
```

```
//Call the function which tests the
//data for errors.
    TestData();
//Errors is a Boolean variable
//which means that it is either true
//or false.
    if (errors) {
            gotoAndStop(2);
    } else {
            gotoAndStop(3);
    }
}
//This function tests the data for
//errors. There are many different
//types of error-checking. These are
//only a few examples of what can
//be done.
function TestData() {
//The following three lines blank out
//the dynamic text boxes labeled
//nameError, emailError, and
//phoneError. These text boxes
//only have messages in them if
//errors are found.
            nameError="";
            emailError="";
            phoneError="";
            errors=true;
//Check to see if the areaCode,
//localExchange, and lastFourNumbers
//are numbers with the proper number
//of digits
            if (areaCode<=100 ||
areaCode>=999){
                    phoneError="Invalid
phone number. Please retype:";
                }
            if (localExchange<=100 ||
localExchange>=999){
                    phoneError="Invalid
phone number. Please retype:";
                }
            if (lastFourNumbers<=1000
|| lastFourNumbers>=9999){
                    phoneError="Invalid
phone number. Please retype:";
                }
//Check to see if the email address
//has an "@" or a "."in it.
            if
(emailAddress.indexOf("@")<=0) {
                    emailError="Invalid
email address. Please retype:";
                }
            if
(emailAddress.indexOf(".")<=2){
                    emailError="Invalid
email address. Please retype:";
                }

if(emailAddress.indexOf("@")>
emailAddress.indexOf(".")+1) {
                    emailError="Invalid
email address. Please retype:";
                }
//See if the name, email
//or telephone number is blank.
            if (name.length==0){
                    nameError="Name is
blank. Please type your name.";
                }
            if
(emailAddress.length==0){
                    emailError="Email
address is blank. Please type your
email address.";
                }
            if (areaCode.length==0 &&
localExchange.length==0 &&
lastFourNumbers.length==0) {
```

```
                    phoneError="Phone
number is blank. Please type your
phone number";
          }
//Check to see if the error messages
//are blank. If so, then
//set errors to false. Otherwise
//errors will be true because
//it was already set to true above.
if (nameError=="" && emailError==""
&& phoneError=="") {
                errors=false;
          }
}
//This is the click handler for the
//start again button on Frame 3.
function StartAgain() {
    gotoAndStop(1);
}
```

The ActionScript tests the following:

- An invalid e-mail address doesn't have an "@"
or a "." in it.
- An invalid area code or local exchange is anything that is not three digits.
- An invalid last four numbers of a phone number is anything that doesn't have four digits.
- A valid name shouldn't be blank.

STEP 5: ADD A BACKGROUND

On Frame 1 of the *background* layer, add any background you want. If necessary, drag the *background*
layer to the bottom of the layer listing. Add a frame
(**F5**) in Frame 3. Lock the layer.

Test the movie and either omit data or put in an
invalid e-mail address or phone number.

COLLAPSIBLE MENU

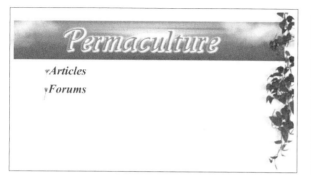

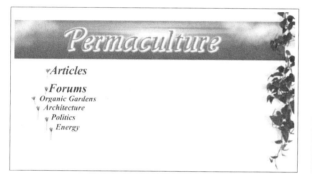
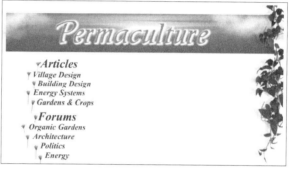

35.1

A collapsible menu lets you expand and collapse a list that contains subheadings. You can look at the expanded menu to view all the subheadings, or you can collapse the menu to view only the main headings.

STEP 1: CREATE BUTTONS FOR MENU ITEMS

For each item on the menu, including submenu items, create a button containing the text you want.

- Start with a new movie. Insert two new layers. Name the three layers *actions*, *menus*, and *background*.
- On the *background* layer (which should be the bottom layer), add any background that you want.
- Choose **Insert ➤ New Symbol**. Make it a button and name it after the name of the first main menu item. Create the button from the text.

> **NOTE**
>
> Find our collapsible menu in **35.fla** in the Techniques folder of the CD-ROM.

- We created a symbol to highlight the button the **Down** frame. First we inserted a new layer. Then we used the Brush tool to draw a stroke, chose **Insert ➤ Convert to Symbol**, and named it *myHighlight*. We placed *myHighlight* over the letters of the button. Be sure to create a solidly filled shape for the **Hit** frame — otherwise, users have to click exactly on the letters to activate the button.
- Continue to make buttons for all the menu and submenu items. For each of the buttons, we inserted a new layer and dragged *myHighlight* onto the **Down** frame of the new layer.
- Click **Scene 1** to return to the main **Timeline**.

STEP 2: ADD ACTIONS FOR THE MENU FRAMES

Each version of the menu is on a separate frame. In our example, containing two menu items, there are four frames—one with both menu items collapsed (closed), one with both expanded (open, that is, showing the submenu items), one with the first menu item expanded, and the fourth with the second menu item expanded.

- Insert keyframes (**F6**) in Frames 2, 3, 4, and 5 of the *actions* layer. Click Frame 2 and open (**Windows ➤ Actions**) or expand the **Actions** panel. Choose **View Options ➤ Expert Mode**. Type the following:

```
stop();
```

- Add the same ActionScript in Frames 3, 4, and 5. (You can copy from Frame 2 and paste it into the other frames.)

> **TIP**
>
> You may want to make the submenu items in a smaller font.

- Click Frame 2 of the *actions* layer. In the **Frame Label** text box of the **Property inspector**, type *CloseClose*. In the same way, label Frame 3 *OpenClose*, Frame 4 *OpenOpen*, and Frame 5 *CloseOpen*.
- Click Frame 1 of the *actions* layer. Type or paste in the following script. (You can copy it from Frame 1 of the *actions* layer of **35.fla** in the Techniques folder of the CD-ROM.

```
item1Open=false;
item2Open=false;
```

STEP 3: ADD ACTIONS FOR THE MENU MOVIE CLIPS

You control the menu by placing your menu items inside a movie clip.

- Choose **Insert ➤ New Symbol**. Make it a movie clip and give it the same name as your first main menu item (*Articles* in our example, **35.fla**). From the **Library** (**Window ➤ Library**), drag in your first main menu item button (*Article*) and center it.
- Select the button that you dragged in and open or expand the **Actions** panel. Type or paste in the following ActionScript.

```
//This code checks to see if the
//submenu for this button
//is open or closed, then directs
//Flash to play a specific frame
//in the main timeline.
```

```
// Item1.open is true if the submenu
//is open, and false if
//the submenu is closed.
on (release) {
//Check to see if this submenu is
//open and if the other submenu is
//open.
    if (_level0.item1Open &&
_level0.item2Open) {
//If so, then set the item1Open
//to false because we will close this
//submenu.
    _level0.item1Open=false;
//Use the with statement to
//target the main timeline.
    with (_root) {
            //Play the frame with the
//code "CloseOpen" which means
//this menu is to appear
//closed and the other menu is to
//appear open.
            gotoAndPlay("CloseOpen");
            }
    } else {
    if (_level0.item1Open==false &&
_level0.item2Open) {
            _level0.item1Open=true;
            with (_root) {

gotoAndPlay("OpenOpen");
            }
    } else {
    if (_level0.item1Open &&
_level0.item2Open==false) {
            _level0.item1Open=false;
            with (_root) {

gotoAndPlay("CloseClose");
            }
    } else {
    if (_level0.item1Open==false &&
_level0.item2Open==false) {
            _level0.item1Open=true;
```

```
    with (_root) {

gotoAndPlay("OpenClose");
            }
        }
    }
}
}
}
}
```

- Click **Scene 1** to return to the main **Timeline**.
- Again create a new movie clip and name it after your second menu item. (Ours is *Forums.*) Drag in the matching button. With the button selected, add the following ActionScript:

```
//This code checks to see if the
//submenu for this button
//is open or closed, then directs
//Flash to play a specific frame
//in the main timeline.
// Item2.open is true if the submenu
//is open, and false if
//the submenu is closed.
on (release) {
//Check to see if this submenu is
//open and if the other submenu is
//open.
    if (_level0.item1Open &&
_level0.item2Open) {
//If so, then set the item1Open //to
false because we will close //this
submenu.
    _level0.item2Open=false;
//Use the with statement to
//target the main timeline.
    with (_root) {
//Play the frame with the code
//OpenClose which means
//this menu is to appear closed and
//the other menu is to
//appear open.
            gotoAndPlay("OpenClose");
```

```
              }
      } else {
      if (_level0.item1Open==false &&
_level0.item2Open) {
              _level0.item2Open=false;
              with (_root) {

gotoAndPlay("CloseClose");
              }
      } else {
      if (_level0.item1Open &&
_level0.item2Open==false) {
              _level0.item2Open=true;
              with (_root) {

gotoAndPlay("OpenOpen");
              }
      } else {
      if (_level0.item1Open==false &&
_level0.item2Open==false) {
              _level0.item2Open=true;
              with (_root) {

gotoAndPlay("CloseOpen");
              }
          }
      }
  }
  }
  }
  }
```

■ Click **Scene 1** to return to the main **Timeline**.

STEP 4: CREATE THE SUBMENUS

Make movie clip symbols for the expanded menus, with the submenus displayed.

■ Choose **Insert** ➢ **New Symbol**. Make it a movie clip named *ArticlesMenu* (or whatever is appropriate for your first main menu item).

■ Drag in the movie clip you created for your first menu item and then drag in the buttons for the submenu items. Position them how you want them to appear when the menu is expanded, as shown in **Figure 35.2**. Click **Scene 1** to return to the main **Timeline**.

■ Choose **Insert** ➢ **New Symbol**. Make it a movie clip named **ForumMenu** (or whatever is appropriate for your second main menu item).

■ Drag in the movie clip you created for your second menu item and then drag in the buttons for its submenu items. Position them how you want them to appear when the menu is expanded. Click **Scene 1** to return to the main **Timeline**.

STEP 5: PLACE THE MENUS ON THE TIMELINE

The various permutations (closed or open) of the menu are each placed in a different frame.

■ Insert keyframes in Frames 2 through 5 of the *menus* layer.
■ Click Frame 2 of the *menus* layer, labeled *CloseClose*. This frame has just the main menu item movie clips, so drag in the movie clips of the main menu items and place them one under the other. See **Figure 35.3**.

35.2

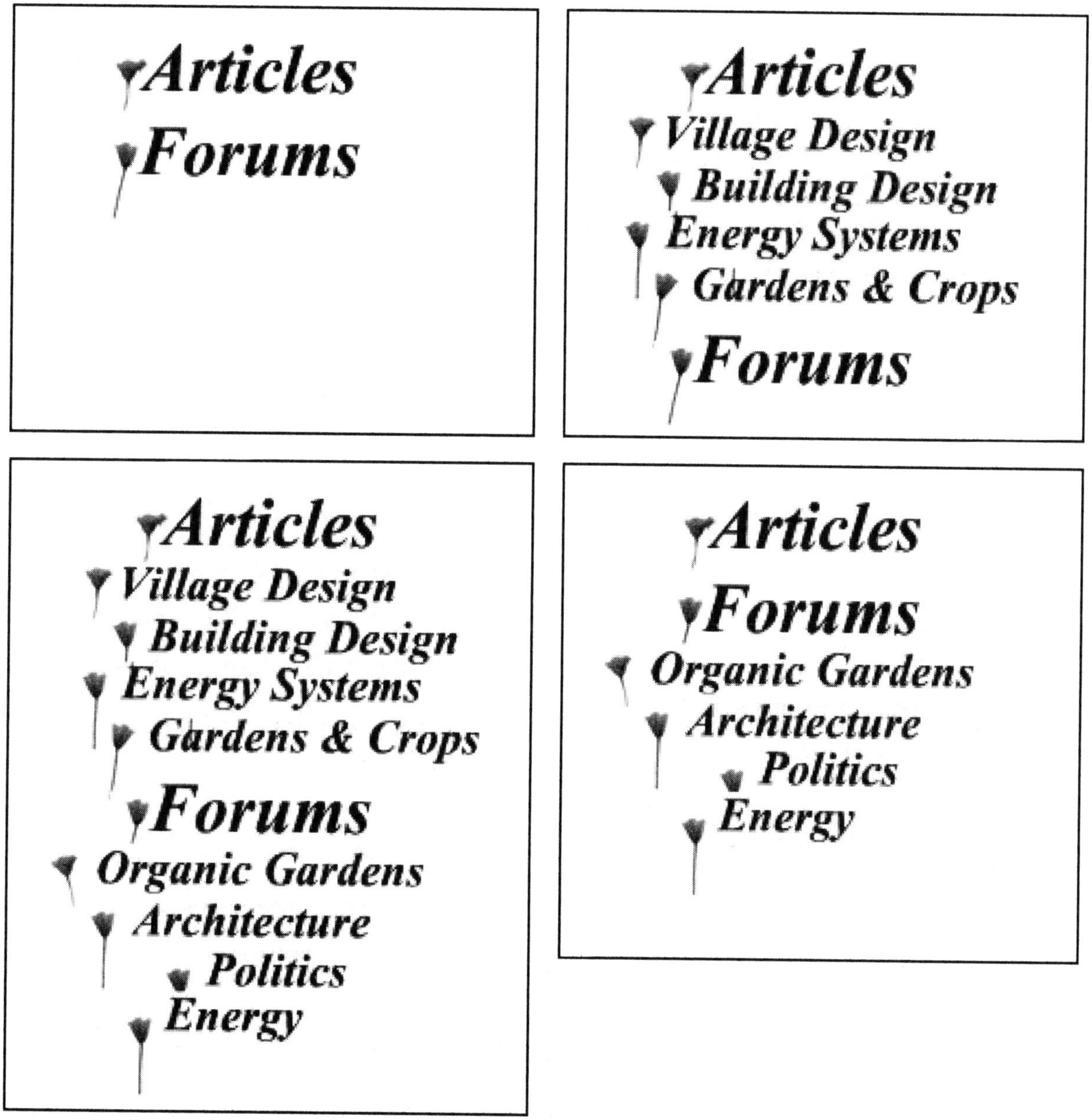

▾*Articles*
▾*Forums*

▾*Articles*
▾*Village Design*
  ▾*Building Design*
  ▾*Energy Systems*
  ▾*Gardens & Crops*
▾*Forums*

▾*Articles*
▾*Village Design*
  ▾*Building Design*
  ▾*Energy Systems*
  ▾*Gardens & Crops*
▾*Forums*
▾*Organic Gardens*
  ▾*Architecture*
    ▾*Politics*
  ▾*Energy*

▾*Articles*
▾*Forums*
▾*Organic Gardens*
  ▾*Architecture*
    ▾*Politics*
  ▾*Energy*

35·3

■ Click Frame 3 of the *menus* layer, labeled *OpenClose*. This frame shows the first menu item expanded and the second one collapsed, so drag in the *ArticlesMenu* movie clip of the first menu item with its submenu items and the *Forum* movie clip (your second main menu item). See **Figure 35.3**.

■ Click Frame 4 of the *menus* layer, labeled *OpenOpen*. This frame shows both menu items expanded, so drag in the *ArticlesMenu* (first menu item with submenus) movie clip and the *ForumMenu* (second menu item with submenus) movie clip. See **Figure 35.3**.

■ Click Frame 5 of the *menus* layer, labeled *CloseOpen*. This frame shows the first item collapsed and the second expanded, so drag in the *Articles* movie clip and the *ForumMenu*. See **Figure 35.3**.

■ Line up all the menus. An easy way is to click **Onion Skin** under the **Timeline** so that you can see Frames 2 through 5 at once.

Test the movie and click the main menu items to expand and collapse the submenus.

3D BOOK AS A USER INTERFACE

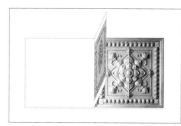

36.1 (CP 23)
Art by Dale Divoky. Used with permission.

A n animation that looks like a book allows the viewer to browse page by page, in a kind of slide show.

STEP 1: CREATE THE LEFT PAGE

Create the left page and the animation that makes the page look like it's turning.

■ Start with a new movie. Draw a rectangle or square with a white fill and a gray stroke. The shape and size should be appropriate for the content that you want to place on the pages.

> **NOTE**
>
> Look for our art gallery in a book in **36.fla** in the Techniques folder of the CD-ROM.

- Choose **Insert** ➤ **Convert to Symbol**. Make it a button named *left-page.*
- Change the name of **Layer 1** to *first left page.* Click Frame 1 and then drag it to Frame 13, to move the *left-page* button to Frame 13.
- With *left-page* still selected, choose the **Free Transform** tool. Drag the transformation point (the small circle in the middle of the rectangle) to the right middle handle, as shown in **Figure 36.2**.
- Insert a keyframe (**F6**) in Frame 24. Select Frames 13 through 24 and choose **Motion** from the **Tween** drop-down list of the **Property inspector** (**Window** ➤ **Properties**).
- Click Frame 13. Choose the **Free Transform** tool and drag the left handle to the right to make the rectangle very narrow. Then drag up on the left side (but not on a handle) to skew the rectangle, as shown in **Figure 36.3**, to create the animation of the left page turning.

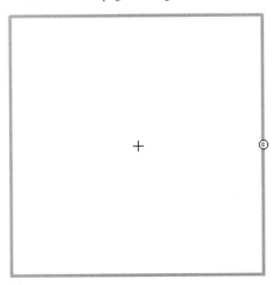

36.2

36.3

STEP 2: CREATE IMAGES FOR THE BOOK

Create pages for the book and make them into buttons.

- Insert a new layer for each page of your book. Name the layers *page1, page2,* and so on, from the top down, so that the top layer is *page1.*
- On each of the layers, draw the image for that page of the book or import images (**File ➢ Import**). For each one, select the image and choose **Insert ➢ Convert to Symbol**. Make them buttons and name them *page1, page2,* and so on. You should now have the *page1* button on the *page1* layer, and so on. Make sure the images are opaque so that they cover the page below.
- Place the images so that they attach to *left-page* and line up. (The images are the right pages.)
- For each page layer, select the image button, choose **Free Transform,** and drag the transformation point to the left handle (which represents the binding of the book).
- For each page layer, select the image button and open (**Window ➢ Actions**) or expand the **Actions** panel. **Choose View Control ➢ Normal Mode.** Choose **Actions ➢ Movie Control** and double-click **play**. The ActionScript should look like the following:

```
on (release) {
    play();
}
```

> **TIP**
>
> Click Onion Skin under the Timeline to help line up the images.

STEP 3: CREATE ANIMATION FOR THE PAGES

Add animation so that each page turns.

- On layer *page1*, insert a keyframe (**F6**) at Frame 12. Select Frames 1 through 12 and choose **Motion** from the **Tween** drop-down list of the **Property inspector**.
- With *page1* selected, choose the **Free Transform** tool and drag the right handle to make the page very narrow and then drag up on the right side (but not on a handle) to skew the page up.
- Click Frame 13 of layer *page1,* **right-click** (Win)/**Ctrl-click** (Mac), and choose **Insert Blank Keyframe** so that the image of the first page disappears. Make sure that this frame and later frames are not tweened. (If they are, select them and choose **None** from the **Tween** drop-down list of the **Property inspector**.) Lock layer *page1* and make it invisible.
- On layer *page2*, insert a keyframe at Frame 24 and another one at Frame 36. Insert a blank keyframe at Frame 37. Select Frames 24 through 36 and choose **Motion** from the **Tween** drop-down list of the **Property inspector**. Click Frame 36 and again make the image narrow and skew it up as you did before. Lock layer *page2* and make it invisible.
- Do the same for the rest of the pages of the book, start each tween 24 frames after the previous one (Page 3 starts on 48, Page 4 starts on 72, and so on).

STEP 4: ADD OTHER LEFT PAGES TURNING

Add the animation for the rest of the left pages turning.

- Insert a new layer, *more left turns.*

> **TIP**
>
> To select the button on the page layer, lock the previous page layers.

- Select Frames 13 through 24 on the *first left turn* layer. Choose **Edit** ➤ **Copy Frames**.
- Click Frame 37 of the *more left turns* layer. Choose **Edit** ➤ **Paste Frames**.
- Click Frame 38 and add a blank keyframe.
- Do the same for all the pages, every 24 pages, on Frames 61, 85, and so on. Add a blank keyframe after each animation.

STEP 5: ADD STOP ACTIONS

Add stop actions at the end of each page turn.

- On the frame after the last frame you use, insert a keyframe. Insert a new layer, *actions*, and add a keyframe on the same frame of the *actions* layer. Open or display the **Actions** panel and double-click **stop**.
- Add a keyframe at the end of each page-turn animation on the *actions* layer (Frames 24, 48, 72, 96, and so on) and add a stop action of each of these keyframes. Also add a stop action in Frame 1 of the *actions* layer.

STEP 6: RETURN TO THE FIRST PAGE

Add actions so that when you click the last page of the book, the book starts at the beginning again.

- On the *more left turns* layer, in Frame 85 (or the beginning of your last animation on that layer), click the turning page button. In the **Actions** panel, double-click **GoTo**. By default, the ActionScript should look like the following:

```
on (release) {
    gotoAndPlay(1);
}
```

- Go to Frame 96 (or the end of your last animation on the *more left turns* layer) and add a **Stop** action there. (Double-click **Stop** in the **Actions** panel.)

Test the movie and click the pages to turn them and leaf through the book.

> **NOTE**
>
> Drag the playhead from Frames 1 through 24 and watch how the animation for the first page segues with the earlier animation you created for the left page turn.

ROLLOVER SCROLLING

37.1
(Photographs by Radim Schreiber. Used with permission.)

A rollover scroll makes text or images scroll when the mouse passes over directional arrows. You can use this technique to create a slide show or marquee.

STEP 1: CREATE THE ARROW BUTTONS

Create the button that will initiate the scrolling motion when the mouse cursor passes over it.

- Start with a new movie. Choose **Insert ➢ New Symbol**. Make it a button and name it *arrow*.
- Create any arrow you want in the **Up** frame. Center it on the **Stage**.
- Insert a keyframe (**F6**) in the **Over** frame and change the color of the arrow.

153

■ Insert a keyframe (**F6**) in the **Hit** frame.
■ Click **Scene 1** to return to the main **Timeline**.
■ Open the **Library** (**Window** ➤ **Library**). Click Frame 1 of the *buttons* layer and drag two instances of *arrow* onto the **Stage**.
■ Select one of the instances and choose **Modify** ➤ **Transform** ➤ **Flip Horizontal**. Position the arrows where you want them on the **Stage**. See **Figure 37.1** for our example.
■ Select the right arrow. Open (**Window** ➤ **Actions**) or expand the **Actions** panel and type or paste in the following ActionScript:

```
on (rollOver) {
    mouseOnRightArrow=true;
}
on (rollOut) {
    mouseOnRightArrow=false;
}
```

■ Select the left arrow. In the **Actions** panel, type or paste in the following ActionScript:

```
on (rollOver) {
    mouseOnLeftArrow=true;
}
on (rollOut) {
    mouseOnLeftArrow=false;
}
```

STEP 2: CREATE A FILMSTRIP

Create a strip of images that you want to scroll.

■ Import your images (**File** ➤ **Import**). Place them end to end. If you want, add some text.

Choose **Insert** ➤ **Convert to Symbol** and make it a movie clip named *myPic* (or *myPicwText*).
■ Position the filmstrip so that the leftmost image is centered horizontally on the **Stage**.
■ In the **Property inspector**, type *myPic* in the **Instance Name** text box.

STEP 3: MAKE A MASK AND BACKGROUND

Make a mask to frame the images in the filmstrip.

■ On the *mask* layer, draw a rectangle the size of the first image and position it over that image.
■ On the *background* layer, draw a rectangle the size of the **Stage**. Your screen should look something like **Figure 37.2**.
■ **Right-click** (Win)/**Ctrl-click** (Mac) the *mask* layer and choose **Mask** to turn the rectangle into a mask.

STEP 4: ADD ACTIONSCRIPT

Add ActionScript to control the scrolling.

■ On the *actions* layer, insert keyframes (**F6**) in Frames 2 and 3. Click Frame 1, and expand or open (**Window** ➤ **Actions**) the **Actions** panel. Type or paste in the following ActionScript. You can find this ActionScript in Frame 1 of the *actions* layer of **37.fla**.

37.2

```
//Initialize variables here.
//Get the image width so you know how
//far to scroll.
    imagewidth=myPic._width;
//myAdjustment adjusts a quirk in
//Flash and is needed to assign the x
//value so it will
//scroll to the proper length.
    myAdjustment=1.0765;
    imagewidthAdjusted=imagewidth
*myAdjustment;
//Initialize the mouseOn...Arrows to
//false.
    mouseOnLeftArrow=false;
    mouseOnRightArrow=false;
//Get the original x location of
//myPic and put it into newX which
//will be a changing variable.
    newX=myPic._x;
//Save the original x location of
//myPic into a variable that will not
//change.
    OrigX=newX;
```

■ In Frame 2 of the *actions* layer, type or paste in the following ActionScript:

```
if (mouseOnLeftArrow){
//imagewidthAdjusted is divided by 2
//because the X position of
//the filmstrip is in the middle of
//the filmstrip, not at the edge.
    if(newX <=
(imagewidthAdjusted/2)){
```

```
//newX is increased by four. If you
//want the filmstrip to move faster
//then increase it by 5 or 6...
        newX=newX+4;
//This statement moves the filmstrip.
        myPic._x =newX;
    }
}
if (mouseOnRightArrow) {
//The if statement keeps the filmstrip
//from scrolling off the page.
    if(newX >= ((origX-
(imagewidth*myAdjustment))/2)){
//newX is decreased by four. If you
//want the filmstrip to move faster
//then decrease it by 5 or 6...
        newX=newX-4;
//This statement moves the filmstrip.
        myPic._x=newX;
    }
}
```

■ In Frame 3 of the *actions* layer, type or paste in the following ActionScript:

```
gotoAndPlay(2);
```

■ Add a Frame (**F5**) in Frame 3 of all the other layers.

TIP

An alternative is to prepare the filmstrip in an image-editing program and import it as one image.

CUSTOM CURSORS

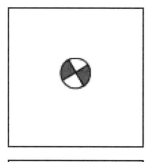

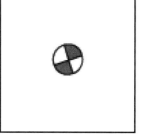

38.1

A cursor is the graphic that shows you where your mouse is pointing. Your operating system comes with several standard cursors, and you may have a choice of additional ones. But suppose you want to create your own cursor for your Web site visitors? You can do this quite easily. You can see a couple of examples shown in **Figure 38.1**. The beach ball is an animation, and the paintbrush is static.

STEP 1: CREATE THE GRAPHIC OR ANIMATION

Create the graphic and animate it if desired.

- Start with a new movie. Use the Flash tools to create the graphic image for your cursor. Remember that cursors should be fairly small.
- Choose **Insert** ➢ **New Symbol**. Assign the movie clip behavior, name it *myMousesym,* and click OK. Delete the symbol on the **Stage**. (It is now in the **Library**.)
- To rotate the symbol, choose **Insert** ➢ **New Symbol**. Give it movie clip behavior and name it *myMouse*. Drag *myMousesym* onto the Stage.

Create a keyframe (**F6**) in Frame 15. Select Frames 1 through 15 and choose **Motion** from the **Tween** drop-down list of the **Property inspector** (**Window** ➢ **Properties**). If necessary, expand the **Property inspector**. From the **Rotate** drop-down list, choose **CW** (or **CCW** to rotate counter-clockwise). Type **1** in the **Times** text box.

■ Choose **Edit** ➢ **Edit Document** to return to the main **Timeline**.

STEP 2: ADD ACTIONSCRIPT

Add ActionScript to make the symbol draggable when you move the mouse.

> **TIP**
>
> When you animate a cursor, make it an animation more or less in place. You don't want the cursor to wander all over the place or your viewers won't know what they're pointing at. An example would be a rotating flower or the revolving beach ball you see in **Figure 38.1**.

■ From the **Library** (**Window** ➢ **Library**), drag the symbol onto the **Stage**. Cut and paste it to center the symbol on the **Stage** or use the **Align** panel (**Window** ➢ **Align**).

■ With the symbol selected, open (**Window** ➢ **Actions**) or expand the **Actions** panel. Click the **View Options** button and choose **Normal** mode.

■ From the **Actions** list, choose **Actions** ➢ **Movie Clip Control**. Double-click **startDrag**. Check the **Lock Mouse to Center** checkbox. Your **Actions** panel should look like **Figure 38.2** when the **startDrag** line is selected.

■ Close or collapse the **Actions** panel.

Test your movie. As you move your mouse, your cursor follows.

> **TIP**
>
> Put your cursor on the top layer of the Timeline so that it moves in front of buttons and other objects on your site.

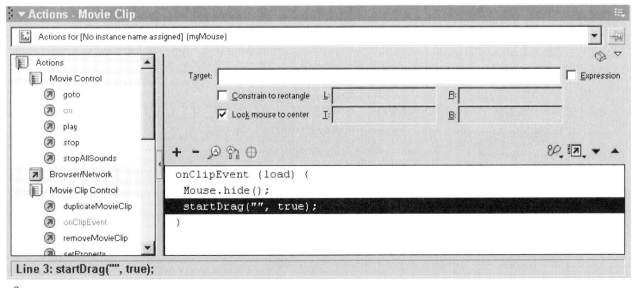

38.2

CASCADING MENU

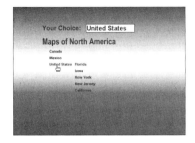

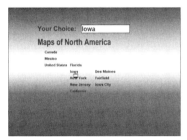

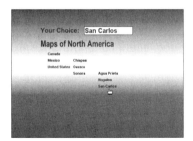

39.1

Create a menu where submenus cascade outward when the mouse is passed over a menu item. When you pass the mouse cursor over the first level of the menu, the second level appears; when you pass the mouse cursor over the second level, the third level appears. We have created a fairly complex system that allows you to have three levels of menus with up to nine choices on each level, for a total of 819 choices! You don't need to use them all — we didn't.

STEP 1: CREATE A BUTTON

Create a button that will contain all the menu options.

■ Start with a new movie. Insert two new layers. Name the three layers *actions, menus,* and *selected text.*

NOTE

You can see our cascading menu in **39.fla** in the Techniques folder of the CD-ROM.

■ Choose **Insert** ➢ **New Symbol**. Make it a button and name it *myButton*. Draw a rectangle with no stroke, 20 pixels high, and wide enough for your widest menu item. (You may need to make an adjustment later.) Center it on the Stage by cutting and pasting it or by using the **Align** panel.

■ With the rectangle selected, open the **Color Mixer** (**Window** ➢ **Color Mixer**) and set the alpha to **10%**. You will eventually set it to **0%**, but for now you need to see the rectangle.

■ Click **Scene 1** to return to the main **Timeline**.

STEP 2: CREATE THE MENU

You use the buttons to create a menu.

■ Choose **Insert** ➢ **New Symbol**. Create a movie clip called *myMenu*. Rename the layer *buttons*.

■ From the **Library** (**Window** ➢ **Library**), drag in *myButton*. Drag in additional instances of *myButton* until you have a tower of them, enough for all your choices on any level and up to a maximum of nine.

■ Select the top button and type *button1* in the **Instance Name** text box of the **Property inspector** (**Window** ➢ **Properties**). Select the next button and give it an instance name of *button2*. Continue to give the rest of the buttons successive names, up to a maximum of *button9*.

■ Insert a new layer and name it *dynamictext*.

■ Create a text box and type some dummy text in it. (The ActionScript doesn't work if you don't.)

■ Select the text box and specify the following settings in the **Property inspector**. You may need to expand the **Property inspector** by clicking its **Expand** arrow.

■ Choose **Dynamic Text** from the **Text Type** drop-down list.

■ Set the size in the **H** and **W** text boxes so that it is exactly the same as the *myButton* rectangle.

■ The **Selectable** button should not be active.

■ The **Show Border Around Text** button should not be active.

■ In the **Var** text box, type *text1*.

■ Place the text box over the top instance of *myButton*.

■ With the text box still selected, copy and paste to make a copy. In the **Var** text box, change the variable to *text2* and place the text box over the next instance of *myButton*.

■ Continue to paste in new copies of the text box, change the variable name to the next value, and place it over the buttons. A bank of three buttons looks like **Figure 39.2**.

STEP 3: ADD ACTIONSCRIPT TO THE BUTTONS

Add ActionScript that controls what happens when the mouse goes over, clicks, or goes off the buttons.

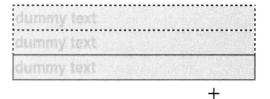

39.2

■ Lock the *dynamic text* layer. Select the first button and open (**Window** ➢ **Actions**) or expand the **Actions** panel. Type or paste in the following ActionScript. You can find it in the *myMenu* symbol of **39.fla** by selecting the topmost button.

```
on (rollOver) {
    if (text1<>""){
    _level0.selectedText=text1;
    mouseOnItem1=true;
    }
}
on (rollOut) {
    mouseOnItem1=false;
}
on (press) {
    mouseClicked=true;
}
```

■ Select the second button. Paste in the same ActionScript, but change **"text1"** to **"text2"** in both (two) locations and change **"mouseOnItem1"** to **"mouseOnItem2"** also in both locations.

■ Do the same for each button, adjusting the ActionScript in the same way to match the number of the button.

■ Click **Scene 1** to return to the main **Timeline**.

STEP 4: COMPILE THE MENU

You compile the menu bank on the main **Timeline**.

■ Click Frame 1 of the *menus* layer. From the **Library**, drag in *myMenu*. In the **Property inspector**, give it an instance name of *menu1* in the **Instance Name** text box.

■ Drag in two more instances of *myMenu* and give them instance names of *menu2* and *menu3*.

■ Line up the three menus next to each other, as shown in **Figure 39.3**.

> **NOTE**
>
> If you change the height of the rectangle, you must also change the buttonHeight value in the second line of ActionScript in Frame 1. See Step 5.

■ Select the first instance of *myMenu*. From the **Color** drop-down list of the **Property inspector**, choose **Alpha** and change the alpha to **0%**. Do the same for the other two instances.

■ Still on the *menus* layer, drag in an instance of *myButton* and place it above the first bank of *myMenu*. With the button still selected, type or paste in the following ActionScript:

```
on (rollOver) {
    mouseOnBox=true;
}
on (rollOut) {
    mouseOnBox=false;
}
```

■ Draw a text box the same size as the button. Type the text that will always appear at the head of the menu. (We used the Maps of North America.) Place the text box over the button. In the **Property inspector**, choose **Static Text** from the **Text Type** drop-down list.

■ On the *selected text* layer, draw a text box at the top of the menu. Specify the following settings in the expanded **Property inspector**:

■ From the **Text Type** drop-down list, choose **Dynamic Text**.

39.3

- In the **Var** text box, type *selectedText*.
- The **Selectable** button should not be active.
- The **Show Border Around Text** button should be active.

STEP 5: ADD ACTIONSCRIPT FOR THE MENU

You now add a considerable amount of ActionScript that defines the menu items and how they work.

- Insert a keyframe (**F6**) in Frame 3 of the *actions* layer. In the **Actions** panel, type the following:

```
gotoAndPlay(2);
```

- In Frame 1 of the *actions* layer, type or paste in the following ActionScript. Then organize the text

that you want on your menu and replace the "c" values with that text. Add "c" statements as needed. We include statements for only three items on each level of the menu. **Figure 39.4** shows a diagram of how the "c" values are structured.

- On the first level of the menu, you can have up to nine menu items. Items for the first level of the menu are multiples of 100. They start with c[100]="c100" and can go up to c[900]="c900";. For example, to add a fourth menu item on the first level, you would insert a line c[400]="c400"; after c[300]="c300";.
- On the second level of the menu, you can also have up to nine menu items for each first level item. Items for the second level of the menu are multiples of 10. The second level menu items are in the same hundred grouping

C100	C110	C111	C112	C113	C119
	C120	C121	C122	C123	C129
	C130	C131	C132	C133	C139
	C190	C191	C192	C193	C199
C200	C210	C211	C212	C213	C219
	C220	C221	C222	C223	C229
	C230	C231	C232	C233	C239
	C290	C291	C292	C293	C299
C300	C310	C311	C312	C313	C319
	C320	C321	C322	C323	C329
	C330	C331	C332	C333	C339
	C390	C391	C392	C393	C399
C900	C910	C911	C912	C913	C919
	C920	C921	C922	C923	C929
	C930	C931	C932	C933	C939
	C990	C991	C992	C993	C999

39.4

as the first level menu items to which they belong. So the second level menu items for your c100 group start with c[110]="c110" and can go up to c[190]="c190";. The second level menu items for your c200 group start with c[210]="c210" and can go up to c[290]="c290";. You can continue up to c[990]="c990" if you have nine first level items.

■   On the third level of the menu, you can also have up to nine menu items for each second level item. Items for the third level of the menu are multiples of 1. The third level menu items are in the same ten grouping as the second level menu items to which they belong. So the third level menu items for your c110 group start with c[111]="c111" and can go up to c[119]= "c119";. The second level menu items for your c210 group start with c[211]="c211" and can go up to c[219]="c219";. You can continue up to c[999]="c999" if you have nine second level items.

```
//Enter the height of your buttons.
buttonHeight=20;
//Put data in your array here.
//Array indexes from 0-99 are
//invalid.
//The values of the array with
//indexes that are multiples of 100
//are
//on the main menu. Values with
//indexes that are multiples of ten
//are on the middle menu and the rest
//are on the third menu.
c = new Array;
c[100]="c100";
c[200]="c200";
c[300]="c300";
c[110]="c110";
c[120]="c120";
c[130]="c130";
c[210]="c210";
c[220]="c220";
c[230]="c230";
c[310]="c310";
c[320]="c320";
c[330]="c330";
c[111]="c111";
c[112]="c112";
c[113]="c113";
c[121]="c121";
c[122]="c122";
c[123]="c123";
c[131]="c131";
c[132]="c132";
c[133]="c133";
c[211]="c211";
c[212]="c212";
c[213]="c213";
c[221]="c221";
c[222]="c222";
c[223]="c223";
c[231]="c231";
c[232]="c232";
c[233]="c233";
c[311]="c311";
c[312]="c312";
c[313]="c313";
c[321]="c321";
c[322]="c322";
c[323]="c323";
c[331]="c331";
c[332]="c332";
c[333]="c333";
```

■ In Frame 2 of the *actions* layer, you need to add a very long ActionScript. Copy and paste this ActionScript from Frame 1 of the *actions* layer of **39.fla** or use the text file on the CD-ROM.

■ Add a frame (**F5**) in Frame 3 of the *menus* and *selected text* layers.

Test the movie and try out the menu.

NOTE

Instead of publishing it in the next few pages of this book, we have placed it in a text file in the Techniques folder of the CD-ROM. Look for **39.txt**.

ANIMATED BUTTON

40.1 (CP 24)

Y ou can animate your buttons. Animated buttons are much more interesting than static buttons, but you need to make sure that they're not confusing.

STEP 1: CREATE THE IMAGE FOR THE BUTTON

Decide how you want your button to work. We created a button that was the same for the Up and Down frames but had an animation for the Over frame. An animation in the Over frame invites the user to pass the cursor over the button and watch the show. But you can do it any way you want.

■ Start with a new movie. Import (**File** ➢ **Import**) or draw any image that you want for the button. This image becomes the static part of the button. We decided on an apple.

> **NOTE**
>
> You can find our animated button in **40.fla** in the Techniques folder of the CD-ROM. This is an animation of an apple being eaten, complete with the sound of biting into the apple.

■ Select the image and choose **Insert** ➢ **Convert to Symbol**. Make it a graphic symbol and name it **Image**.

■ Delete the symbol from the **Stage**. (It's in the **Library**.)

STEP 2: CREATE THE ANIMATION

Create the animation part of the button.

■ Choose **Insert** ➢ **New Symbol**, make it a movie clip, and name it *mcOver*. (In our example, we created the animation for the **Over** frame of the button.)

■ Create any animation you want. You may want to use the graphic symbol that you created (in Step 1) as a basis for your animation. In that case, drag it onto the **Stage** and animate it. Ideally, you want an animation that doesn't move around too much.

■ Click **Scene 1** to return to the main **Timeline**.

STEP 3: CREATE THE BUTTON

Here you create the button, using the animation you just created (in Step 1).

> **NOTE**
>
> Of course, if you want all the frames of the button (Up, Over, and Down) to be animated, you can skip this step. However, you may still want to start with a symbol as a basis for the animation.

■ Choose **Insert** ➢ **New Symbol**, make it a button and name it *btnImage*.

■ Drag the graphic symbol or movie clip that you want from the **Library** (**Window** ➢ **Library**) to the **Stage**. Center it by cutting and pasting it or by using the **Align** panel (**Window** ➢ **Align**).

■ Insert a keyframe (**F6**) in the **Over** frame. If you want the **Up** and **Over** frames to be different, delete the symbol on the **Stage** (that is automatically carried over from the **Up** frame). Drag the graphic symbol or movie clip that you want from the **Library** (**Window** ➢ **Library**) to the Stage. Center it by cutting and pasting it or by using the **Align** panel (**Window** ➢ **Align**).

■ Repeat for the **Down** frame.

■ Insert a keyframe (**F6**) in the **Hit** frame. If the shape of the **Up** frame symbol is suitable for the **Hit** frame (large and simple enough), you don't need to do anything more. However, if you have complex, moving animation, delete the symbol on the **Stage** and draw a square or circle that covers the area well and is large enough for viewers to click easily.

■ Click **Scene 1** to return to the main **Timeline**.

STEP 4: PLACE THE BUTTON ON THE STAGE

From the Library, drag an instance of *btnImage* onto the **Stage**. Test your movie (you can't test the button on the **Stage**) and play with the button to see the animation.

> **NOTE**
>
> When you create the animation, if you want to add a sound, insert a **sound** layer and choose **File** ➢ **Import** to import the sound.

PRELOADER WITH PROGRESS DISPLAY

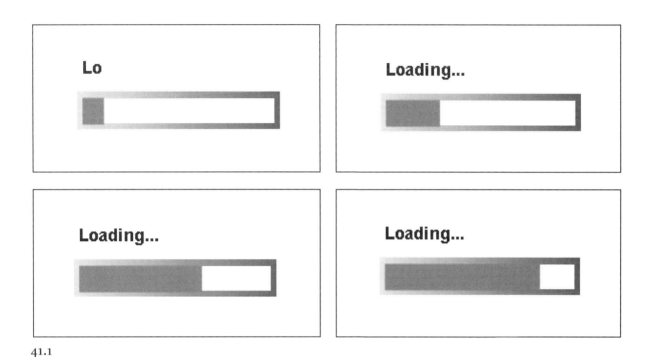

41.1

An almost universal Flash technique, a preloader shows the viewer how much of the movie has been loaded. Of course, it's better to make your Flash movies small, so your viewers don't have to wait at all. But, for when you're overly ambitious. . . .

STEP 1: CREATE THE PRELOADER BOX

You create the rectangles needed to display the progress display.

- Start with a new movie. Insert two new layers. Name the top one *progressbar,* the middle one *whitespace,* and the bottom one *outerbox.*
- On the *outerbox* layer, draw a long, thin, filled rectangle.
- On the *whitespace* layer, draw a white filled rectangle that is slightly narrower and shorter than the first rectangle. In the bottom section of

the **Property inspector** (**Window** ➤ **Properties**), note the white rectangle's height in the **H** text box and its **X** location in the **X** text box. With the white rectangle selected, choose **Insert** ➤ **Convert to Symbol**. Make it a movie clip named *whiteSpace*. In the **Instance Name** text box of the **Property inspector**, name it *whiteSpace*.

■ On the *progressbar* layer, draw a rectangle filled with a third color. It needs to be the same height as the *whitespace* rectangle and 10 pixels wide. Make any necessary adjustments in the **H** and **W** text boxes of the **Property inspector**. It should be at the same X location as the white rectangle. Choose **Insert** ➤ **Convert to Symbol**. Make it a movie clip named *myProgressBar*. In the **Instance Name** text box of the **Property inspector**, name it *myProgressBar*. Your preloader box should look similar to **Figure 41.2**

STEP 2: CREATE THE PRELOADER ANIMATION

Create some animation that repeats over and over while your movie is loading. We use a simple animation that displays the letters LOADING... one after another.

■ Insert a new layer and name it *loading*. Type the word **LOADING...** above the preloader box.

41.2

■ With the letters selected, choose **Modify** ➤ **Break Apart** and then **Modify** ➤ **Distribute to Layers**.

■ On the **O** layer, click Frame 1 and drag it to Frame 3, so that the O appears when the animation gets to Frame 3. On the **A** layer, click Frame 1 and drag it to Frame 5. Continue this process with each successive layer, each time dragging Frame 1 to a higher frame, staggering the appearance of each letter.

■ Click Frame 24 on the **L** layer, scroll down to the last **.** (period) layer, press **Shift**, and click Frame 24 on the last period layer to select Frame 24 on all the letter layers. Press **F5** to insert a frame.

■ Also add a keyframe (**F6**) on Frame 24 of the *progressbar*, *whitespace*, and *outerbox* layers.

STEP 3: ADD ACTIONSCRIPT

You use ActionScript to set the location of the progress bar, test to see if all the frames are loaded (when the main movie will play), program the width of the progress bar, and loop the preloader animation.

■ Insert a new layer and name it *actions*.

■ In Frame 1 of the *actions* layer type or paste in the following ActionScript. (You can find it in Frame 1 of the *actions* layer of the **Preloader Scene** of **41.fla**.)

> **NOTE**
>
> Find our preloader in **41.fla** in the Techniques folder of the CD-ROM. You may find that this loads too quickly on your hard drive to see the preloader. To stream the movie more slowly, test the movie and choose **View** ➤ **Show Streaming**. Then click the Debug menu and choose a streaming rate.

```
//Assign the original value of xLoc.
//myProgressBar must originally be
//only 10 pixels wide and it is
//properly placed in the
//inner box of the progress display.
xLoc = myProgressBar._x;
```

■ Insert a keyframe (**F6**) in Frame 2 of the *actions* layer and type or paste in the following ActionScript. (You can find it in Frame 2 of the *actions* layer of the **Preloader Scene** of **41.fla**.)

```
//Test to see if all the frames are
//loaded. If so, leave the preloader
//and go to the main scene.
if (_framesloaded >= _totalframes) {
    gotoAndPlay ("Main", 1);
}
//The following line defines the
//fraction of the movie that is
//loaded.
fractionLoaded =
_framesloaded/_totalframes;
//The inner progress box will be the
//width of the whiteSpace
//when the fraction loaded is 1. The
//extra 2 pixels give us a margin of
//error so no white space is exposed
//when the frames are completely
//loaded.
myProgressBar._width =
(fractionLoaded*whiteSpace._width) +
2;
// Five pixels must be subtracted
//from new _x of the progress bar
//because
//the original progress bar was 10
//pixels wide and the new _x needs to
//compensate
//for that original width.
myProgressBar._x = xLoc +
(fractionLoaded *
whiteSpace._width/2) - 5;
```

■ Insert a keyframe in Frame 24 of the *actions* layer and type or paste in the following ActionScript. (You can find it in Frame 24 of the *actions* layer of the **Preloader Scene** of **41.fla**.)

```
gotoAndPlay(2);
```

STEP 4: CREATE THE SCENES AND MAIN MOVIE

You need to put the preloader in a separate scene from the main movie.

■ **Choose Window** ➤ **Scene** to open the **Scene** panel. Double-click the scene name (by default Scene 1) and type *Preloader*.

■ Click the **Add Scene** button. Name the new scene **Main**. Make sure that the **Preloader** scene is on top.

■ Create your main movie. It can be anything you want. The main movie should either loop or stop at the end so that it doesn't replay the preloader. To loop a movie, add the following in the last frame:

```
gotoAndPlay(1);
```

To stop a movie, add the following in the last frame:

```
Stop();
```

Test the movie.

SLIDE SHOW WITH SPECIAL EFFECTS TRANSITIONS

42.1 (CP 25)
(Art by Dale Divoky. Used with permission.)

Flash is often used for slide shows. Here we create the structure for a slide show with two types of cool transitions between slides.

STEP 1: SET UP THE SLIDES

Import or create your slides and put them in the Library as symbols.

- Start with a new movie. Insert three new layers. Name the four layers, from the top down, *button, effects, slides,* and *actions.*
- Create your slides by using the Flash drawing tools or by importing images. We imported four images. Each slide needs to be saved as a movie clip. Name them *slide1, slide2, slide3,* and *slide4.* In each movie clip, insert a new layer, name it *background,* and drag it to the bottom of the layer list. On the *background* layer, create an opaque rectangle the same size as the **Stage**.

STEP 2: CREATE A "NEXT" BUTTON

Add a button that navigates from slide to slide.

- Choose **Insert** ➤ **New Symbol**. Make it a button and name it *NextSlide*. When you're done, click **Scene 1** to return to the main **Timeline**.
- Click Frame 1 of the *button* layer. Drag a copy of *NextSlide* from the **Library (Window** ➤ **Library)** onto the **Stage**.

STEP 3: INSERT THE SLIDES

Insert the slides into the slide show. You start with Slide 2 now because you will be creating the effect of Slide 1 dissolving or wiping into Slide 2 and so on.

- On the *slides* layer, insert a keyframe (**F6**) every 20 frames so that you have a keyframe for each slide. For example, if you have four slides, insert a keyframe in Frames 21, 41, and 61. You already have the default keyframe in Frame 1.
- Click Frame 1 on the *slides* layer and drag in *slide2* from the **Library**. Click Frame 21 and drag in *slide3*. Continue in this way, ending with *slide1*.

STEP 4: ADD SOME ACTIONS

You add actions to control the slides and program the button.

- Insert a keyframe in Frame 2 of the *actions* layer. Open (**Window** ➤ **Actions**) or expand the **Actions** panel. Choose **View Options** ➤ **Normal Mode**.

- Click Frame 1 of the *actions* layer. In the **Actions** panel, choose **Actions** ➤ **Movie Control** and double-click **Stop**.
- Insert keyframes in Frames 40, 41, 60, 61, and so on of the *actions* layer.
- Add a **Stop** action in Frames 40, 60, and so on.
- In the last keyframe, double-click **GoTo**. In the **Frames** text box, type **2** so that the ActionScript reads:

```
gotoAndPlay(2);
```

- Select the button. In the **Actions** panel, double-click **Play**, so that the ActionScript reads:

```
on (release) {
    play();
}
```

STEP 5: CREATE THE EFFECTS LAYER

You insert the slides again into the *effects* layer, this time in the proper order.

- Click Frame 1 of the *slides* layer. (Remember that this is *slide2*.) Choose **Edit** ➤ **Copy Frames**. Click Frame 21 of the *effects* layer and choose **Edit** ➤ **Paste Frames**.
- Click Frame 21 of the *slides* layer. Copy the frame and paste it into Frame 41 of the *effects* layer. Continue for all the slides except the last one.
- Click the last keyframe of the *slides* layer, which is your first slide. Copy the frame and paste it into Frame 1 of the *effects* layer.

STEP 6: CREATE THE TRANSITION EFFECTS

You now create the dissolve or wipe effects. For the dissolve:

- On the *effects* layer, insert a keyframe in the last frame for each slide, before each existing keyframe, at Frames 20, 40, and so on.
- Select Frames 1 through 20. From the **Property inspector's Tween** drop-down list, choose **Motion**. Click Frame 20, then click the *slide1* movie clip. From the **Property inspector Color** drop-down list, choose **Alpha** and set the alpha to **0%**.
- Do the same with Frames 21 through 40, and so on. Play the animation, and you'll now see how each slide dissolves into the next.
- On the *button* layer, insert a frame (**F5**) at the last frame of your animation.

For the wipe effect:

- Insert a new layer above the *effects* layer. Name it *mask*.
- Insert a keyframe on Frame 20 of the *effects* layer.
- On Frame 1 of the *effects* layer, draw a filled rectangle the size of the **Stage**.
- Select Frames 1 through 20 and choose **Shape** from the **Tween** drop-down list of the **Property inspector**.
- Click Frame 20. Select the rectangle and choose the **Free Transform** tool. Drag the right middle handle to the left until you have only a thin line on the left side of the **Stage**.
- Select Frames 1 through 20 and choose **Edit** ➢ **Copy Frames**. Paste these frames on the *effects* layer at Frames 21, 41, and so on. (If necessary, select any unnecessary tweened frames that are created at the end and choose **Edit** ➢ **Clear Frames**.)

- On the *button* layer, insert a frame (**F5**) at the last frame of your animation.

Test your movie to watch the slide show.

7

MINI-APPLICATIONS

Y ou can use ActionScript to program environments that are small applications in their own right. You can combine programming and Flash MX animation to provide your viewers with lots of fun!

Technique 43 shows you how to create a news ticker. The text that scrolls across the screen comes from an outside source. You can use the same technique for advertising, stock prices, weather, or for any continually changing content. Technique 44 teaches you how to make both an analog and a digital clock.

The next three techniques are for music lovers only. Technique 45 shows you how to create a keyboard and a synthesizer. Using the keyboard or buttons on the screen, users create music and play it back. In Technique 46, you find out how to make an MP3 player, offering controls to play, stop, and control the volume of the music. And finally, Technique 47 shows you how to create a drum set that enables users to create rhythms on various types of drums. Turn up the volume!

In Technique 48, we turn to art with a simple onscreen paint program. Let your viewers paint up a storm. Then, for the mathematically minded, Technique 49 offers a calculator. Finally, in Technique 50, we explain how to create a stand-alone Flash movie that you can put on a CD-ROM or even on a disk.

NEWS TICKER

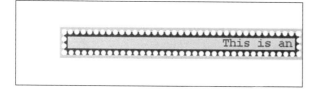

43.1 (CP 26)

Text in a news ticker scrolls across the screen continually. The source of the text is always an outside file. You can use the news ticker for news, sports scores, stock market results, ads, a thought for the day, your current special offer, or anything else you want.

STEP 1: CREATE THE TEXT

The text comes from a text file. First you create this file.

■ Use **Notepad** (Win)/**SimpleText** (Mac) to create the file. Decide how wide in characters you want your ticker to be. Start the file with **tickerText=** and then add almost as many spaces as your number of characters. You need the spaces so that the text starts to appear at the right side of the ticker window; otherwise, it disappears before viewers can read it. However, if you use more spaces than you have characters, the ticker never starts! We started with 48 spaces for a 50-character ticker.

■ Continue your text without pressing Enter/Return except if you want the ticker to start a new line. If you want to start a new line, you need to add spaces before that line as you did before the first line.

■ End the file with as many spaces as the number of your characters. For example, if your ticker is 50 characters wide, end with 50 spaces. See **Figure 43.2** for our example.

■ Save the file as *myTickerText.txt* and close the file.

> **NOTE**
>
> Look for **43.fla** in the Techniques folder of the CD-ROM as well as **myTickerText.txt.** These two files work together to create the news ticker. They must be in the same folder.

STEP 2: ADD ACTIONSCRIPT

You add ActionScript to control the ticker.

■ Start with a new movie in Flash. Insert a new layer. Name the top layer *actions* and the bottom layer *ticker.*

■ Insert a keyframe (**F6**) in Frames 2 and 3 of the *actions* layer.

■ In Frame 1 of the *actions* layer, type or paste in the following ActionScript:

```
//This loads variables from the text
//file myTickerText.txt which needs
//to be in the same folder as the
//Flash movie. The variable that it
//loads into is the same variable
//that is set in the text file. In
//this case the variable is
//"tickerText".

loadVariables("myTickerText.txt","")
;
i=1;
```

■ In Frame 2 of the *actions* layer, type or paste in the following ActionScript:

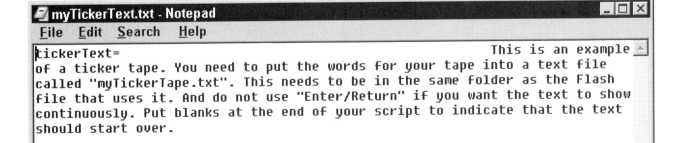

```
tickerText=                                This is an example
of a ticker tape. You need to put the words for your tape into a text file
called "myTickerTape.txt". This needs to be in the same folder as the Flash
file that uses it. And do not use "Enter/Return" if you want the text to show
continuously. Put blanks at the end of your script to indicate that the text
should start over.
```

43.2

```
//Take a 50 character slice of
//tickerText and put it into
//myTickerText which is the
//variable for the dynamic text box.
text1=tickerText.slice(i,i+50);
//Increment i so that the next 50
//character slices will be one
//character offset.
i=i+1;
//Check to see if myTickerText is
//blank. You need to put blanks in
//the end of your text file to
//indicate it
//is at the end. Also, you need to
//put blanks in the beginning so that
//the text does not jump onto the
//screen when it starts. But make
//sure that the text at the beginning
//is less than 50 blanks. Otherwise
//this statement will cause your
//ticker tape to stop before it even
//begins.
if (text1=="
"){
    gotoAndPlay(1);
}
```

■ In Frame 3 of the *actions* layer, type or paste in the following ActionScript:

```
gotoAndPlay(2);
```

STEP 3: CREATE THE TEXT BOX

Add the dynamic text box.

■ In Frame 1 of the *ticker* layer, draw a text box. With the text box selected, specify the following settings in the **Property inspector** (**Window ➤ Properties**):

- ■ From the **Text Type** drop-down list, choose **Dynamic Text**.
- ■ From the **Font** drop-down list, choose **_typewriter**. Traditionally, tickers use this font (although you don't have to).
- ■ In the **Var** text box, type *text1*.
- ■ If you want a border around the ticker, click the **Show Border Around Text** button.
- ■ The **Selectable** button should not be active.

■ In Frame 3 of the *ticker* layer, insert a frame (**F5**).

If you want, you can add a *background* layer, drag it to the bottom, and draw a rectangle to create a framing effect around the ticker or add any artwork you want. We also added a *marqee* layer to create the lights.

Test your movie to watch the text scroll across the screen.

TIP

To create a text box the right width, create a static text box just below the dynamic text box and enter the number of characters you want to show. Then change the width of the dynamic text box to match the width of the static text box.

DIGITAL OR ANALOG CLOCK

44.1 (CP 27)

Sunday, June 23, 2002

44.2 (CP 27)

Y ou can place a realistic looking digital or analog clock on your site. Both show the day and date as well. We start with the digital clock, shown in **Figure 44.1**.

DIGITAL CLOCK

The digital clock is in **44a.fla** in the Techniques folder of the CD-ROM.

STEP 1: CREATE A SYMBOL WITH ACTIONSCRIPT

Create a movie clip and add ActionScript that defines the time, day, and date.

- Start with a new movie. Choose **Insert** ➢ **New Symbol**. Make the symbol a movie clip and call it *Digital Clock*.

■ Insert a new layer. Name the top layer *actions* and the other layer *digital clock*.

■ Insert a keyframe (**F6**) into Frame 2 of the *actions* layer. Type or paste in the following ActionScript.

```
myDate=new Date();
myHours=myDate.getHours();
myMinutes = myDate.getMinutes();
myAMPM = "PM";
if (myHours < 12) {
myAMPM = "AM";
}
if (myHours>=12) {
            myHours = myHours-12;
}
mySeconds = myDate.getSeconds();
if(myMinutes < 10) {
    myTime = myHours + ":0"
+myMinutes;
} else {
myTime = myHours + ":" + myMinutes;
}
weekdays =
["Sunday","Monday","Tuesday",
"Wednesday","Thursday","Friday",
"Saturday"];
months =
["January","February","March",
"April","May","June","July",
"August","September","October",
"November","December"];
myDateVar =
weekdays[myDate.getDay()] + ", "
+ months[myDate.getMonth()] + " "
+ myDate.getDate() + ","
+ " " + myDate.getfullYear();
gotoAndPlay(1);
```

■ Click Frame 1 of the *digital clock* layer. Use the **Text** tool to create a text box for the time. Open or expand the **Property inspector** and then choose

> **NOTE**
>
> To find the ActionScript in **44a.fla** on the CD-ROM, open the **Library** (**Window** ➤ **Library**) and double-click *Digital Clock*. Then click Frame 2 of the *actions* layer and open the **Actions** panel (**Window** ➤ **Actions**).

Dynamic from the **Text Type** drop-down list. In the **Var** text box of the **Property inspector**, type *myTime*.

■ Create another, narrower dynamic text box for the seconds. In the **Var** text box, call it *mySeconds*.

■ Create a third dynamic text box wide enough for the day and date. In the **Var** text box, call it *myDateVar*.

■ On the *digital clock* layer, insert a frame (**F5**) in Frame 2.

■ Click **Scene 1** to return to the main **Timeline**.

STEP 2: CREATE THE CLOCK

You draw the clock and bring an instance of the *Digital Clock* movie clip onto the Stage.

■ Insert a new layer and call it *date and time*. Name the existing layer *clock*.

■ On Frame 1 of the *clock* layer, draw your clock.

■ Click Frame 1 of the *date and time* layer. From the **Library**, drag an instance of *Digital Clock* onto the clock you drew.

Test your movie and check out the day, date, and time.

ANALOG CLOCK

The analog clock is programmed similarly to the digital clock but adds ActionScript to control the rotation of the hands. You also have to draw the hands.

NOTE

See our digital clock in **44a.fla** in the Techniques folder of the CD-ROM. The analog clock is **44b.fla**.

STEP 1: CREATE THE HANDS

Draw the hour, minute, and second hands.

■ Start with a new movie. Choose **Insert** ➢ **Symbol** and create a movie clip named *Clock1*. Insert four new layers. From the top down, name the five layers *actions, Secondhand, Minutehand, Hourhand,* and *Date*.

■ On the *Secondhand* layer, draw your second hand in the vertical (12 o'clock) position. Don't worry about the size relative to the clock right now. Place the second hand so that its bottom is at the middle of the symbol (on the registration point).

■ Copy and paste the second hand to duplicate it. (See Note.) Select the duplicate second hand and open the **Color Mixer** panel (**Window** ➢ **Color Mixer**). In the **Alpha** text box, type *0*. Place the transparent second hand in the 6 o'clock position so that you have a second hand that is twice as long as your original hand, as shown in **Figure 44.3**

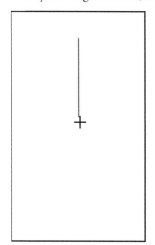 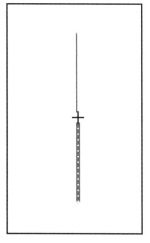

44·3

(with the second hand unselected and then with both pieces selected).

■ Select both pieces of the second hand and choose **Insert** ➢ **Convert to Symbol**. Make it a movie clip and call it *Secondhand*. With *Secondhand* selected, type *seconds1* in the **Instance Name** text box of the **Property inspector**. Lock the *Secondhand* layer.

■ On the *Minutehand* layer, draw the minute hand in the 12 o'clock position. Place it so that the bottom of the minute hand is at the middle of the clock. Duplicate it and rotate it 180 degrees if it is wider at its base. Make the duplicate transparent and place it in the 6 o'clock position, as you did with the second hand. Convert both parts to a movie clip named *Minutehand*. With *Minutehand* selected, type *minutes1* in the **Instance Name** text box of the **Property inspector**. Lock the *Minutehand* layer.

■ On the *Hourhand* layer, draw the hour hand in the 12 o'clock position. Follow the same procedure as for the minute and second hands, duplicating it, making the duplicate transparent, placing it, and converting it to a movie clip named *Hourhand*. With *Hourhand* selected, type *hours1* in the **Instance Name** text box of the **Property inspector**. Lock the *Hourhand* layer.

STEP 2: ADD THE DATE/TEXT BOX

You add a dynamic text box for the date.

■ On the *Date* layer, use the **Text** tool to create a dynamic text box, by choosing **Dynamic** from the **Text Type** drop-down list of the **Property inspector**. In the **Var** text box (expand the **Property inspector** if necessary), type *myDate1*. Place it low enough to leave room for the clock.

STEP 3: ADD ACTIONSCRIPT

Add ActionScript to get the time and date and control the rotation of the hands.

■ In Frame 2 of the *actions* layer, add a keyframe (**F6**).

■ Type or paste in the following ActionScript. You can find this ActionScript in Frame 2 of the *actions* layer of the *Clock1* symbol in **44b.fla**.

```
//Get the date, hours and minutes.
myDate=new Date();
myHours=myDate.getHours();
myMinutes = myDate.getMinutes();
//Convert to 12 hours instead of 24
if (myHours>=12) {
                myHours = myHours-12;
}
mySeconds = myDate.getSeconds();
//Rotate the hours by 30 degrees, the
//minutes by 6 degrees
//and the seconds by 6 degrees.
setProperty("hours1",_rotation,
myHours*30+(myMinutes/2));
setProperty("minutes1",_rotation,
myMinutes*6);
setProperty("seconds1",_rotation,
mySeconds*6);
//Convert the number returned by the
//getDay function to the
//actual weekday.
weekdays =
["Sunday","Monday","Tuesday",
"Wednesday","Thursday","Friday",
"Saturday"];
```

```
months = ["January","February",
"March","April","May","June","July",
"August",
"September","October","November",
"December"];
myDate1 = weekdays[myDate.getDay()] +
", " + months[myDate.getMonth()] +
"" + myDate.getDate() + ","
 + " " + myDate.getfullYear();
gotoAndPlay(1);
```

■ Select Frame 2 of all the other layers and add a frame (**F5**).

■ Unlock any locked layers. Select all the layers and choose **Insert** ➢ **Convert to Symbol**. Make it a movie clip named *Clock1*.

■ Click **Scene 1** to return to the main **Timeline**.

STEP 4: DRAW THE CLOCK

■ Insert a new layer. Name the top layer *hands*. Name the other layer *clock*. On the *Clock* layer, draw your clock (minus the hands) and center it by cutting and pasting it or by using the **Align** panel (**Window** ➢ **Align**). Lock the *Clock* layer.

■ From the **Library** (**Window** ➢ **Library**) drag in the *Clock1* symbol. If necessary, resize the hands to fit the clock (or vice versa).

MUSIC KEYBOARD AND SYNTHESIZER

45.1 (CP 28)

By clicking the Flash buttons (that look like a piano keyboard) or keys on the computer keyboard, you can play a tune.

STEP 1: CREATE THE PIANO KEYBOARD

You start by creating the graphics of the keyboard.

■ Start with a new movie. Use Flash's drawing tools to draw a white key. We used a simple rectangle filled with a white and gray gradient. Choose **Insert** ➤ **Convert to Symbol**. Make it a button named *WhiteKey*. Delete *WhiteKey* from the **Stage** — it's in the **Library**.

■ Draw the black key. We used a rectangle filled with a black and white gradient. Convert it to a button symbol named *BlackKey*. Delete *BlackKey* from the **Stage**.

185

■ Insert three new layers. From the top down, name the four layers *BlackKeys, WhiteKeys, PianoDetail,* and *Piano.*

■ Click Frame 1 of the *BlackKey* layer and drag the *BlackKey* button onto the **Stage**. Continue to drag instances of *BlackKey* onto the **Stage** until you have as many as you want. (You need five black keys for one octave and ten for two octaves.)

■ Click Frame 1 of the *WhiteKey* layer and drag in as many instances of the *WhiteKey* button as you need (which is eight white keys for one octave and 15 for two octaves).

■ Use the **Align** panel (**Window** ➢ **Align**) to line up and distribute the keys. Place the black keys over the white keys as they appear on a piano keyboard. (See **Figure 45.1**.)

■ On the *Piano* layer, draw a rectangle to represent the piano. We used a blue/dark blue radial gradient.

■ On the *PianoDetail* layer, we added two dark lines for shadows above and below the keys.

STEP 2: IMPORT THE SOUNDS

You need a sound for each note. You can record them yourself if necessary. Be sure to remove any "dead" sound before and after the note, using Flash's sound editing tools or tools in another sound editing program.

NOTE

Try out **45.fla** in the Techniques folder of the CD-ROM. Click the keyboard buttons or press the computer keys to play a tune. Look at Figure 45.2 to see how the computer keys correspond to the piano keys.

■ Import sounds (**File** ➢ **Import**) for each key you have drawn. Be sure to distinguish between different octaves of the same note when you name the files, for example, MiddleC and HighC. You can find our sounds in the Techniques folder of the CD-ROM, from LowC to HighC.

■ In the **Library** (**Window** ➢ **Library**), right-click each sound and choose **Linkage**. In the **Linkage Properties** dialog box, click **Export for ActionScript**. The sound's name should be in the **Identifier** text box. If it is not, type the same name as the sound. Click **OK**.

STEP 3: ADD ACTIONSCRIPT

You need to add ActionScript to each button.

■ Select each button and change it to a movie clip by choosing **Movie Clip** from the **Symbol Behavior** drop-down list of the **Property inspector**. Then add the following ActionScript in the **Actions** panel (**Window** ➢ **Actions**).

```
onClipEvent(load){
    mySound=new Sound();
//Enter the name of your sound
//below. It must be in the symbol
//library and linked for export to
// the ActionScript.

    mySound.attachSound("D");
}
on (press) {
    mySound.start();

}
//Enter the key that you wish to use
//for this sound below.
on (keyPress "x") {
    mySound.start();
}
```

■ Be sure to change the ActionScript for each movie clip so that it refers to the appropriate sound and key on the computer keyboard. For the "keyPress" expression, you need to decide which computer keys will correspond with the piano keys. We used the arrangement shown in **Figure 45.2**.

Test your movie and either click the buttons or press the appropriate keys on your computer keyboard. Make some music!

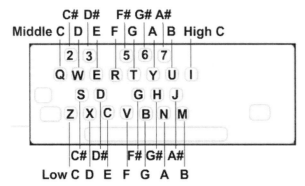

45.2

MP3 PLAYER

46.1 (CP 29)
Thanks to Joseph Rienstra (`www.chira.com/j`*)
for the music.*

The MP3 player plays MP3 sounds. You can add your own sounds to the playlist. You can play, rewind, fast-forward, and stop/pause. You can adjust the volume and pan the sound between the speakers. You can choose the song either from the drop-down list or from the Track slider.

STEP 1: CREATE THE ARTWORK

You start by creating the artwork for the MP3 player.

■ Start with a new movie. Insert six new layers and name the seven layers from the top down: *actions, counter, slider, triangle, buttons, comboBox, player.*
■ On the *player* layer draw the background for the player. It can be a simple rectangle. Lock this layer.

NOTE

Look for our MP3 player in **46.fla** in the
Techniques folder of the CD-ROM.

- Click the *comboBox* layer. Choose **Window** ➢
Components and drag a **ComboBox** onto the
top portion of the MP3 player, as shown in
Figure 46.1. Use the **Free Transform** tool to
resize it if necessary. Open (**Window** ➢
Properties) and expand the **Property inspector**.
In the **Instance Name** text box, type *SongList*.
On the **Parameters** tab, set the **Editable** property
to **False**. Click the **changeHandler** row and type
whichSong. Click the **Labels** row and then the
button at the right end of the row to open the
Values dialog box, shown in **Figure 46.2**. Click
the plus sign, click the *defaultValue* name, and type
in the name of an MP3 file. Continue to add all the
MP3 files you want in your playlist. Click **OK**.
- On the *Buttons* layer, draw a covering for the
comboBox with an alpha of *20*, to hide it. Include
the down arrow in your artwork.

STEP 2: ADD THE BUTTONS

Add the pause, play, reverse, and forward buttons.
Add the sliders.

- Choose **Insert** ➢ **New Symbol**. Make it a button called *buttons*. Draw the artwork for one button that you will use for the Stop, Rewind, Play,
and Fast Forward buttons. Click **Scene 1** to return
to the main **Timeline**.
- Choose **Insert** ➢ **New Symbol** again. Make it
a movie clip called *Volume*. Insert a layer and
name the two layers *slider* (the top layer) and *bar*.
Draw the slider on the *slider* layer. Ours is just a
tall, thin rectangle with a black and white linear

gradient and is 102 pixels high. (See Warning.)
Drag in the *buttons* button onto the *slider* layer
and resize the button, so it isn't as tall. Place it at
the bottom of the slider. With the button selected,
choose **Movie Clip** from the **Property inspector's
Symbol Behavior** drop-down list to change the
button to a movie clip. Click **Scene 1** to return to
the main **Timeline**.
- In the **Library** (**Window** ➢ **Library**), select
the *Volume* movie clip. **Right-click** (Win)/
Ctrl-click (Mac) and choose **Duplicate**.
Rename it *Tracks*.
- In the **Library** (**Window** ➢ **Library**), select the
Volume movie clip. **Right-click** (Win)/**Ctrl-click**
(Mac) and choose **Duplicate**. Rename it *Pan*.
Double-click *Pan* to edit it. Select the slider button
(it will show a blue line around it — don't double-
click it or you will edit the *buttons* symbol). Move
it up so that it is vertically centered on the bar, as
you can see in **Figure 46.1**. (Panning moves the
sound between the left and right speakers, so you
want it to start in the middle.)
- Drag four instances of *buttons* onto the **Stage**
and position them. From the left, type the following instance names in the **Instance Name** text box
of the **Property inspector**: *myStop, myRewind,
myPlay, myFastForward*. Also drag the sliders
Volume, Tracks, and *Pan* onto the Stage and position them on the player.
- On the *triangle* layer, add triangles and a symbol
for the **Pause/Stop** button, as shown in **Figure 46.1**.
Also add any labels that you want for the sliders
and the MP3 player as a whole.

NOTE

The MP3 files must be in the same folder as the
movie if you don't include the path.

STEP 3: ADD THE COUNTER

You add a counter to measure the progress of the music or sounds.

- On the *counter* layer, use the **Text** tool to make a text box. In the **Property inspector**, choose **Dynamic Text** from the **Text Type** drop-down list. Also in the **Property inspector** (expanded), make the **Selectable** button not active and the **Show Border Around Text** button active.
- Set the font, size, and color for the text that will go in the counter. Right-justify the text.
- In the **Var** text box, type *myCounter*.

STEP 4: ADD THE ACTIONSCRIPT

Add the ActionScript to control the entire MP3 player in the first five frames and for each of the buttons and sliders.

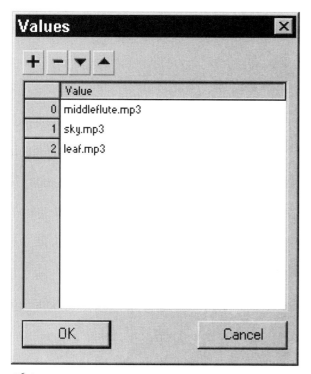

46.2

- On the *actions* layer, put keyframes (**F6**) in Frames 2 through 5.
- Select Frame 5 in all the other layers and add a frame (**F5**).
- In Frame 1 of the *actions* layer, type or paste in the following ActionScript, which you can find in Frame 1 of the *actions* layer of **46.fla** on the CD-ROM:

```
playing=false;
mySound = new Sound();
whichSong();

//This function is called by the
//changehandler of the comboBox.
// It loads the selected MP3 file and
//if the sounds are playing, then it
//plays it and causes the counter to
//show by going to Frame 2. If
//the music is not playing, then it
//goes to Frame 4 which
//sets the counter to 0.
function whichSong(){
myIndex=SongList.getSelectedIndex();
    mySong=
SongList.getItemAt(myIndex).label;
    mySound.loadSound(mySong,false);
    myPosition=0;
    if (playing) {
```

```
            mySound.start();
            gotoAndPlay(2);
        }
    if (playing==false) {
    gotoAndPlay(4);
        }
}
//This function is called in Frame 2
//in the OnSoundComplete function.
//It increments the index of the
//comboBox and selects the next
//sound.
//When the comboBox is incremented, it
//calls the changeHandler, whichSong.
function nextSong() {
    myPosition=0;
    if
(myIndex==SongList.getLength()-1) {
        myIndex=0;
    } else {
        myIndex=myIndex+1;
    }

SongList.setSelectedIndex(myIndex);
myStop.onRelease =function () {
    playing=false;
    myPosition = mySound.position;
    mySound.stop();
}
myRewind.onRelease = function() {
    if (playing==false) {
        myPosition=0;
        gotoAndPlay(4);
    }
    if (playing) {
        mySound.stop();
        myPosition =
mySound.position - 5000;
        if (myPosition<=0) {
```

```
            myPosition=0;
        }
mySound.start(myPosition/1000,1);
    }
}
//Start the sound playing.
myPlay.onRelease = function() {
    if (playing==false) {

mySound.start(myPosition/1000,1);
    playing=true;
    gotoAndPlay(2);
    }
}
myFastForward.onRelease=function() {
    if (playing==false) {
myPosition=myPosition+5000;
        if
(myPosition>=mySound.duration) {
myPosition=mySound.duration;
        }
    gotoAndPlay(4);
    }
    if (playing) {
        mySound.stop();
        myPosition =
mySound.position + 5000;
        if
(myPosition>=mySound.duration) {
myPosition=mySound.duration-5000;
        }
mySound.start(myPosition/1000,1);
    }
}
```

■ In frame 2 of the *actions* layer, type or paste in the following ActionScript, which you can find in frame 2 of the *actions* layer of **46.fla** on the CD-ROM:

```
//Frames 2 and 3 set and reset the
//counter.
myCounter=math.round(mySound.
Position/1000);

//this function is called when the
//sound is complete.
//It goes to the next sound and
//restarts playing.
mySound.onSoundComplete = function()
{
    nextSong();
    mySound.start();
    gotoAndPlay(3);
}
```

■ In Frame 3 of the *actions* layer, type or paste in the following ActionScript, which you can find in Frame 3 of the *actions* layer of **46.fla** on the CD-ROM:

```
//This sets the counter
myCounter=math.round(mySound.
position/1000);
gotoAndPlay(2);
```

■ In Frame 4 of the *actions* layer, type or paste in the following ActionScript, which you can find in Frame 4 of the *actions* layer of **46.fla** on the CD-ROM:

```
//The counter shows the new position
//set by the fast forward or
// reverse buttons while the sound
//is not playing.
myCounter=math.round(myPosition/1000
);
```

■ In Frame 5 of the *actions* layer, type or paste in the following ActionScript, which you can find in Frame 5 of the *actions* layer of **46.fla** on the CD-ROM:

```
gotoAndPlay(4);
```

■ The leftmost slider controls the volume. You need to attach the ActionScript to the movie clip of the slider itself (an instance of *buttons*), not to the *Volume* symbol. Double-click the *Volume* symbol to edit it and select the *buttons* movie clip. Type or paste in the following ActionScript, which you can find by double-clicking the *Volume* symbol in **46.fla** on the CD-ROM and then selecting the slider movie clip (*buttons*).

```
onClipEvent(load){
//Enter the height of the slider
//below;
    sliderHeight=102;
//myY is the position of the slider
//button.
//The button must be positioned at
//the bottom of the slider to start.
    myY=_y;
    top=_y-(sliderHeight/2);
    bottom= _y+(sliderHeight/2);
    right=_x;
    left=_x;
    m=new sound;
    m.setPan(0);
}
on(press){

startDrag("",false,left,top,right,
bottom);
}
on(release){
    stopDrag();
    m.setPan(
(myY-_y)*200/sliderHeight);
}
```

■ The middle slider pans the sound between the speakers. Double-click the *Pan* symbol to edit it and select the *buttons* movie clip. Type or paste in the following ActionScript, which you can find by double-clicking the *Pan* symbol in **46.fla** on the CD-ROM and then selecting the slider movie clip (an instance of *buttons*).

```
onClipEvent(load){
//Enter the height of the slider
//below:
    sliderHeight=102;
//myY is the position of the slider
//button. The button must be
//positioned at the bottom
//of the slider to start
    myY=_y;
    top=_y-(sliderHeight/2);
    bottom= _y+(sliderHeight/2);
    right=_x;
    left=_x;
    m=new sound;
    m.setPan(0);
}


on(press){

startDrag("",false,left,top,right,
bottom);
}
on(release){
    stopDrag();
    m.setPan(
(myY-_y)*200/sliderHeight);
    }
```

■ The right slider chooses the track, that is, the item of music or sound that plays. Double-click the *Track* symbol to edit it and select the *buttons* movie clip. Type or paste in the following ActionScript, which you can find by double-clicking the *Track* symbol in **46.fla** on the CD-ROM and then selecting the slider movie clip (an instance of *buttons)*.

```
onClipEvent(load){
//Enter the height of the slider
//below:
    sliderHeight=102;
//myY is the position of the slider
//button.
//The button must be positioned at
//the bottom of the slider to start
    myY=_y;
    top=_y-sliderHeight;
    bottom= _y;
    right=_x;
    left=_x;
    numberOfSongs=
_root.SongList.getLength();
}


on(press){

startDrag("",false,left,top,right,
bottom);
}
on(release){
    stopDrag();

myIndex=math.round(numberOfSongs*(((
myY-_y)*100/sliderHeight)/100));
_root.SongList.setSelectedIndex
(myIndex)
;
    }
```

Test the movie and play some music!

DRUM SET

47.1 (CP 30)

C reate a drum set for your viewers to play. Kids love it, and so do teenagers. Their parents? We're not so sure.

STEP 1: CREATE THE DRUMHEAD

You start by drawing the drumhead, which is the basis for all the drums.

- Start with a new movie. Add two layers. On the bottom layer, draw a circle. We use a radial gradient from beige to white. On the middle layer, draw a slightly larger circle — ours is brown. On the top layer, draw a slightly larger circle for the rim. Ours has a linear gradient from brown to gold.

- Choose **Insert** ➢ **Convert to Symbol**. Make it a graphic symbol named *DrumHead*.
- Delete the two additional layers you made.

STEP 2: CREATE THE SNARE DRUM

You create the first complete drum.

- Choose **Insert** ➢ **Symbol**. Make it a button named *DrumSideView*.
- Drag in *DrumHead* and use the **Free Transform** tool to turn it into an oval by dragging inward on the top or bottom handle.
- Draw a rectangle to create the side of the drum. You can make the top and bottom curves by using the **Envelope** option of the **Free Transform** tool.

TIP

Another way to create the side of the drum is to break apart *DrumHead* (**Modify** ➢ **Break Apart**) and place it over the top of the rectangle. Deselect the drumhead and drag it away from the rectangle to cut out the top curve. To cut out the bottom curve, select the rectangle and copy it to the Clipboard. Paste it back onto the **Stage**. Drag the original rectangle onto the bottom of the new rectangle, deselect it, and drag it off to cut out the bottom curve.

- Use a flattened version of the side to create the rims and narrow rectangles to create the poles from one rim to the other. Add fills or gradients.

STEP 3: PLACE THE DRUMS ON THE STAGE

You place copies of the drums on the Stage and draw stands for them.

- From the **Library**, drag several instances of *DrumSideView* onto the **Stage**. Use the **Free Transform** tool to resize and rotate them as desired.
- Draw stands for the drums. You can use rectangles and fill them with a gradient.

STEP 4: DRAW THE BASE DRUM AND CYMBAL

Draw the bass drum based on the drumhead and draw a cymbal.

- Choose **Insert** ➢ **New Symbol**. Make it a button named *DrumFrontView*.
- Draw two circles the same size as *DrumHead* and place them so that they almost completely overlap. These are the side and the back rim of the drum. See the bass drum in **Figure 47.1**. Center these circles.
- Drag *DrumHead* onto the **Stage** from the **Library** and place it slightly lower and to the left of the circles.
- Add rectangles or lines to connect the front and back of the drum.
- Fill the drum with the same gradients as the snare drum.
- Click **Scene 1** to return to the main **Timeline**.

■ Choose **Insert** ➤ **New Symbol**. Make it a button named *Cymbal*.

■ Draw an oval with the **Circle** tool. Give it a green and white radial gradient. Copy the oval, resize it to about 50%, and put the smaller version in the middle of the original.

■ Click **Scene 1** to return to the main **Timeline**.

STEP 5: IMPORT THE SOUNDS

Import the sounds for the drums. You can record sounds if you wish. You can also use our sounds, which are in the Techniques folder on the CD-ROM.

■ Choose **File** ➤ **Import** and import the sounds into the **Library**.

■ Select each sound in the **Library**. **Right-click** (Win)/**Ctrl-click** (Mac) and choose **Linkage**. In the **Linkage Properties** dialog box, choose **Export for ActionScript** and click **OK**.

STEP 6: ADD ACTIONSCRIPT

Add ActionScript to play the sounds when the mouse passes over the drums.

■ Select each button instance on the **Stage** individually. For each one, choose **Movie Clip** from the **Symbol Behavior** drop-down list in the **Properties inspector**.

■ Add the following ActionScript to each movie clip instance. For each one, change the sound in the "mySound.attachSound" expression and the key that users can press in the "keyPress" expression. We use the letters a, s, d, f, r, e, w, and g.

```
onClipEvent(load){
    mySound=new Sound();
    mySound.attachSound("snare");
}
on (rollOver) {
    mySound.start();
}
on (keyPress "a") {
    mySound.start();
}
```

Test the movie and move the cursor over the drums. Happy drumming!

ON-SCREEN PAINT PROGRAM

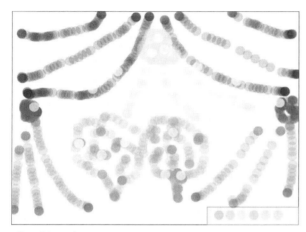

48.1 (CP 31)

O ur on-screen paint program puts splashes of color on the canvas. You won't be able to draw a masterpiece, but it's lots of fun.

STEP 1: MAKE THE BUTTONS

The circles are buttons that you click to choose your color.

- Start with a new movie. Insert four new layers and name the five layers, from the top down, *actions, Brush, Paint, PaintBorder,* and *Canvas.*
- On the *paint* layer, draw a small circle (see **Figure 48.1**) with no stroke in any color you want. Copy and paste it six times, dragging each to a new location so the circles don't cover each other up. Use the **Paint Bucket** tool to change the color of each circle so that you have seven

different colors. As you select the color from the **Fill Color** box, note the hexadecimal number in the **Color** box and write it down. (You'll need it later.) Use the **Color Mixer** (**Window** ➢ **Color Mixer**) to change the alpha of the circles to **20%**.

■ Select each circle and choose **Insert** ➢ **Convert to Symbol**. Make it a button. Name the buttons *BlueDot, RedDot,* and so on, depending on the colors you chose.

■ Place the circles along the bottom-right corner of the **Stage**, as shown in **Figure 48.1**.

■ On the *canvas* layer, draw a rectangle with a stroke and a fill to create a border around the circles. Choose **Ctrl+X** (Win)/**⌘+X** (Mac) to cut the fill. (You paste it back in a minute.)

■ Also on the *canvas* layer, draw a rectangle the size of the **Stage**. Choose **Edit** ➢ **Paste in Place** to paste the fill of the small rectangle. Deselect the fill and then select it again and press **Del** to delete the fill. Doing this cuts out the rectangle from the larger rectangle.

■ Select the large rectangle and choose **Insert** ➢ **Convert to Symbol**. Make it a button named *Canvas.*

■ On the *brush* layer, drag in any one of the circles from the **Library** (**Window** ➢ **Library**). In the **Property inspector** (**Window** ➢ **Properties**), choose **Movie Clip** from the **Symbol Behavior** drop-down list to change the button to a movie clip. In the **Instance Name** text box of the **Property inspector**, type *trail1*. This button will be invisible so you can place it anywhere. It determines the shape that is drawn on the canvas.

NOTE

Play around with our paint program in **48.fla** in the Techniques folder of the CD-ROM.

TIP

Another option is to make one *dot* button, drag in seven copies, and change their color and alpha using the **Property inspector**.

STEP 2: ADD ACTIONSCRIPT

You add ActionScript to control the paint program.

■ Select the *Canvas* button. Open (**Window** ➢ **Actions**) or expand the **Actions** panel and type or paste in the following ActionScript, which you can find by selecting the *Canvas* button in **48.fla**.

■ Select each dot button and type or paste in the following ActionScript into the **Actions** panel. Note that you must change the six digits after "Ox" in the "setRBG" expression to match the hexadecimal color of each button.

```
on (release) {
    myColor=new Color(trail1);
    myColor.setRGB(0x0000FF);
}
```

■ On the *actions* layer, insert keyframes (F6) in Frames 2 through 4.

■ In Frame 1, type or paste in the following ActionScript. (You can find it in Frame 1 of the *actions* layer of **48.fla**.)

```
i=1;
trail1._visible=false;
```

■ In Frame 2, type or paste in the following ActionScript. (You can find it in Frame 2 of the *actions* layer of **48.fla**.)

```
stop();
```

■ In Frame 3, type or paste in the following ActionScript. (You can find it in Frame 3 of the *actions* layer of **48.fla**.)

```
duplicateMovieClip("trail1",
"myPaint" add i,i);
    setProperty("myPaint" add
i,_visible,true);
//Set the x,y position of the
//mousetrails according to the
//previous x,y positions of the
//mouse.

setProperty("myPaint"+i,_x,_xmouse);

setProperty("myPaint"+i,_y,_ymouse);
i = i + 1;
```

■ In Frame 4, type or paste in the following ActionScript. (You can find it in Frame 4 of the *actions* layer of **48.fla**.)

```
gotoAndPlay(3);
```

■ Select Frame 4 of all the other layers and press **F5** to add a frame.
■ Double-click the frame rate box at the bottom of the **Timeline** and change the frame rate to 30 or 60 for faster responsiveness.
Test the movie, choose a color and drag the mouse all over the canvas to draw.

TIP

To change the shape of *trail1*, break it apart and change its shape. Then choose **Insert** ➤ **Convert to Symbol**, name it *trail1* and give it the instance name of *trail1*.

CALCULATOR

49.1 (CP 32)

T his calculator is functional and fun. It also makes a great educational tool.

STEP 1: CREATE THE ARTWORK

Start by drawing the buttons and labeling them.

- Start with a new movie. Insert three new layers. Name the four layers from the top down *actions, TextBox, Button labels,* and *Buttons.*
- Choose **Insert** ➤ **Create Symbol**. (We used a Stage size of 350 by 480 pixels. To change the Stage size, choose **Modify** ➤ **Document**.) Make it a button named *key*. Draw the button on the **Up** frame. When you're done, click **Scene 1** to return to the main **Timeline**.

NOTE

Look for our calculator in **49.fla** in the Techniques folder of the CD-ROM.

■ Decide on the configuration of your buttons. On the *Buttons* layer, drag in one row of *key* from the **Library** (**Window** ➢ **Library**). Use the **Align** panel (**Window** ➢ **Align**) to line up and distribute the buttons evenly. Then select them and copy them to make more rows. Distribute the rows evenly.

■ On the *Button labels* layer, add labels to your buttons. Align the labels. Lock the *Button labels* layer.

■ Select each of the *key* buttons and give it an instance name according to its label, as follows:

```
"0"=my0
"1"=my1
"2"=my2, and so on through 9
". " = myDecimal
"+"=myPlus
"-"=myMinus
"*"=myTimes
"/"=myDivide
"="=myEquals
"Clear"=myClear
"Clear Entry"=myClearEntry
```

STEP 2: ADD THE TEXT BOX

The text box displays the numbers and the results of the calculations.

■ At the top of the calculator create a text box on the *TextBox* layer. From the **Text Type** drop-down list of the **Property inspector**, choose **Dynamic Text**. Also in the Property inspector, make the **Selectable** button active and the **Show Border**
Around Text box inactive. In the **Var** text box, type *myNumber*.

■ Choose **Insert** ➢ **New Symbol**. Make it a movie clip named *FakeZero*. Use the **Text** tool to create a zero. Set the desired size, font, and color. Click **Scene 1** to return to the main **Timeline**.

■ On the *TextBox* layer, drag in an instance of *FakeZero*. In the **Instance Name** text box of the **Property inspector**, type *myFakeZero*.

■ On the *Buttons* layer, create some artwork to border the text box.

STEP 3: ADD ACTIONSCRIPT

The ActionScript defines each button and its function.

In Frame 1 of the *actions* layer, type or paste in the following ActionScript. You can find it in Frame 1 of the *actions* layer of **49.fla**.

```
myOp="";
lastNumber=0;
thisNumber=0;
myNumber="";
newNum=true;
my1.onRelease= function () {
    numberPress(1);
}
my2.onRelease= function () {
    numberPress(2);
}
my3.onRelease= function () {
    numberPress(3);
}
my4.onRelease= function () {
    numberPress(4);
}
my5.onRelease= function () {
    numberPress(5);
}
my6.onRelease= function () {
    numberPress(6);
}
```

```
my7.onRelease= function () {
    numberPress(7);
}
my8.onRelease= function () {
    numberPress(8);
}
my9.onRelease= function () {
    numberPress(9);
}
myDecimal.onRelease= function () {
    numberPress(".");
}
my0.onRelease= function () {
    numberPress(0);
}


function numberPress(whichKey) {
    if (newNum) {

setProperty("myFakeZero",_visible,
false);
        myNumber=string(whichKey);
    } else {

myNumber=myNumber+string(whichKey);
    }
    newNum=false;
}


myPlus.onRelease= function () {
    myOperator("add");
}
function myOperator(myNewOp) {
    thisNumber=Number(myNumber);
    if (myOp=="add") {

myNumber=lastNumber+thisNumber;
        thisNumber=myNumber;
    }
    if (myOp=="subtract") {
```

```
        myNumber=lastNumber-
thisNumber;
        thisNumber=myNumber;
    }
    if (myOp=="times") {

myNumber=lastNumber*thisNumber;
        thisNumber=myNumber;
    }
    if (myOp=="divide") {

myNumber=lastNumber/thisNumber;
        thisNumber=myNumber;
    }
    lastNumber=thisNumber;
    newNum=true;
    myOp=myNewOp;
}
myMinus.onRelease= function () {
    myOperator("subtract");
}
myTimes.onRelease= function () {
    myOperator("times");
}
myDivide.onRelease= function () {
    myOperator("divide");
}
myClear.onRelease= function() {
    myOp="";
    lastNumber=0;
    thisNumber=0;
    myNumber="";
    newNum=true;
    setProperty("myFakeZero",
_visible,
true);
}
myClearEntry.onRelease = function() {
    myNumber="";
    newNum=true;
    setProperty("myFakeZero",
_visible,
```

```
true);
}
myEquals.onRelease=function() {
    thisNumber=Number(myNumber);
    newNum=true;
    if (myOp=="add") {
    myNumber=lastNumber+thisNumber;
    }
    if (myOp=="subtract") {
        myNumber=lastNumber-
thisNumber;
    }
    if (myOp=="times") {

myNumber=lastNumber*thisNumber;
    }
    if (myOp=="divide") {

myNumber=lastNumber/thisNumber;
    }
    lastNumber=0;
myOp="";
}
```

Test the movie and try adding up some numbers.

CREATE A STAND-ALONE MOVIE

50.1

You can create a Flash movie that plays on its own without the Flash player. It's called a *projector,* and you use it when you want to put your movie on a CD-ROM or even a diskette. On Windows, the projector creates an .exe file. On the Mac, you get an .hqx file. Either way, all you need to do is double-click the file to play it.

STEP 1: PUBLISH THE MOVIE

Publish a projector file.

- Open any existing movie. Choose **File ➤ Publish Settings**.
- In the **Publish Settings** dialog box, uncheck any checked boxes and check **Windows Projector**, **Macintosh Projector**, or both.
- Click **Publish and** then click **OK**. Flash saves the file in the same folder as the original movie.

> **NOTE**
>
> **50.exe and 50 Projector are stand-alone movies
> of our drum set for Windows and the Mac. (See
> Technique 47.)**

STEP 2: PLAY THE MOVIE

Burn the file to a CD-ROM or copy it to a floppy disk.

- If you want the projector file on a CD-ROM,
  you need to burn it onto a CD, using the instructions for your CD-burning software. Otherwise,
  copy it to a disk (if it's small enough to fit).
- To play the movie, double-click the file.

> **NOTE**
>
> **If you use a Windows computer to create a Mac
> projector, you need to use a file translator, such
> as BinHex, so that the Mac Finder recognizes the
> file as an application.**

APPENDIX A
WHAT'S ON THE CD-ROM

This appendix provides you with information on the contents of the CD that accompanies this book. For the latest and greatest information, please refer to the ReadMe file located at the root of the CD. Here is what you will find:

- System Requirements
- Software Installation Instructions
- What's on the CD
- Troubleshooting

SYSTEM REQUIREMENTS

Make sure that your computer meets the minimum system requirements listed in this section. If your computer doesn't match up to most of these requirements, you may have a problem using the contents of the CD.

FOR WINDOWS 98 SE, WINDOWS 2000, WINDOWS NT4 (WITH SP 4 OR LATER), WINDOWS ME, OR WINDOWS XP:

- PC with a Pentium processor running at 200 Mhz or faster
- At least 64MB of total RAM installed on your computer; for best performance, we recommend at least 128MB
- 1024 x 768, 16-bit (thousands of colors) color display or better
- A CD-ROM drive

FOR MACINTOSH:

- Mac OS computer running Mac OS 9.1 and higher or OS X 10.1 and higher
- At least 64MB of total RAM installed on your computer; for best performance, we recommend at least 128MB
- 1024 x 768, 16-bit (thousands of colors) color display or better
- CD-ROM drive

SOFTWARE INSTALLATION INSTRUCTIONS (WINDOWS)

To install a particular piece of software, open its folder with My Computer or Windows Explorer. What you do next depends on what you find in the software's folder:

1. First, look for a ReadMe.txt file or a .doc or .htm document. If this is present, it should contain installation instructions and other useful information.

2. If the folder contains an executable (.exe) file, this is usually an installation program. Often it will be called Setup.exe or Install.exe, but in some cases the filename reflects an abbreviated version of the software's name and version number. Run the .exe file to start the installation process.

SOFTWARE INSTALLATION INSTRUCTIONS (MACINTOSH)

To install a particular piece of software, double-click the icon of its folder. What you do next depends on what you find in the software's folder:

1. First, look for a Read Me file or a .htm or .html document. If this is present, it should contain installation instructions and other useful information.

2. To open a program that comes with an installer, double-click the Install or Installer icon.

WHAT'S ON THE CD

The following sections provide a summary of the software and other materials you'll find on the CD.

50 TECHNIQUES

All the techniques from the book, including Flash FLA files, Flash movies (SWF files), code listings, and supplemental files, are on the CD in the folder named Techniques.

APPLICATIONS

The following applications are on the CD:

Shareware programs are fully functional, trial versions of copyrighted programs. If you like particular programs, register with their authors for a nominal fee and receive licenses, enhanced versions, and technical support. *Freeware programs* are copyrighted games, applications, and utilities that are free for personal use. Unlike shareware, these programs do not require a fee or provide technical support. *GNU software* is governed by its own license, which is included inside the folder of the GNU product. See the GNU license for more details.

Trial, demo, or evaluation versions are usually limited either by time or functionality (such as being unable to save projects). Some trial versions are very sensitive to system date changes. If you alter your computer's date, the programs will "time out" and will no longer be functional.

Acrobat Reader, from Adobe, Inc., freeware. For more information, go to `www.adobe.com/products/acrobat/main.html`. Acrobat Reader allows you to view and print files in Adobe's Portable Document Format (PDF), including the electronic version of this book included on the CD-ROM.

Flash MX, from Macromedia, Inc., trial version. For more information, go to `www.macromedia.com/software/flash` If you don't already own Flash MX, here it is in all its glory for you to try out. You can use this trial version to explore all the Flash techniques in this book and to build your own Flash movies.

Photoshop Elements, from Adobe, Inc., trial version. For more information, go to `www.adobe.com/products/photoshopel/main.html`. Photoshop Elements is Adobe's powerful digital imaging software package designed to be easy-to-use by hobbyists, amateur photographers, and business users.

EBOOK VERSION OF *50 FAST FLASH TECHNIQUES*

The complete text of this book is on the CD in Adobe's Portable Document Format (PDF). Now you can take it along with you on your laptop, wherever you may roam. You can read and search through the file with the Adobe Acrobat Reader (also included on the CD). Adobe Acrobat Reader allows you to view our book on your computer, with all the layout, fonts, links, and images just as they appear in the paper version of the book.

TROUBLESHOOTING

If you have difficulty installing or using any of the materials on the companion CD, try the following solutions:

- **Turn off any anti-virus software that you may have running.** Installers sometimes mimic virus activity and can make your computer incorrectly believe that it is being infected by a virus. (Be sure to turn the anti-virus software back on later.)
- **Close all running programs.** The more programs you're running, the less memory is available to other programs. Installers also typically update files and programs; if you keep other programs running, installation may not work properly.
- **Reference the ReadMe:** Please refer to the ReadMe file located at the root of the CD-ROM for the latest product information at the time of publication.

If you still have trouble with the CD, please call the Customer Care phone number: (800) 762-2974. Outside the United States, call 1 (317) 572-3994. You can also contact Wiley Customer Care by e-mail at `techsupdum@wiley.com`. Wiley will provide technical support only for installation and other general quality control items; for technical support on the applications themselves, consult the program's vendor or author.

APPENDIX B

OTHER RESOURCES

Visit this book's companion Web site, `www.wiley.com/legacy/compbooks/Finkelstein`, for more Flash techniques and resources. Click the link for *50 Fast Flash MX Techniques* and find out about:

- Updates to this book
- "50 Techniques" Readers' Gallery

View the work of other readers and share your best work, too! If you have created a great Flash technique that you want to share with others, please e-mail the FLA file to `flashtechniques@ellenfinkelstein.com` along with a step-by-step explanation of how to create the technique, using the same structure as the book. If we can reproduce the technique using your instructions, we may post it on our site. We may also use your technique in future editions of this book (with your permission and with credit to you).

- A useful list of online Flash resources, including places to find other techniques

You can contact the authors by e-mail if you have any questions about the book. Contact Gurdy Leete at `gleete@mum.edu`. Contact Ellen Finkelstein at `ellenfinkl@bigfoot.com`. Ellen's Web site is `www.ellenfinkelstein.com`. Please note that we cannot guarantee that we will answer all our e-mail, although we do read it all. Also, we cannot provide technical support for Flash.

ABOUT THE AUTHORS

Ellen Finkelstein has written numerous best-selling computer books on AutoCAD, PowerPoint, and Flash. She also teaches courses in these programs as well as others and recently taught a course in Web writing. The three editions of her *AutoCAD Bible* have sold more than 50,000 copies. Her previous book was *Flash MX For Dummies*, also co-written with Gurdy Leete.

Gurdy Leete has been teaching computer art and animation for 10 years at Maharishi University of Management, where he is assistant professor of digital media. Prior to joining the faculty there, he worked as a computer animator for Doug Henning, the renowned magician. He holds B.F.A. and M.F.A. degrees in Filmmaking from the San Francisco Art Institute. His award-winning short films have been shown nationally, and he is also an award-winning software engineer.

CONTRIBUTING AUTHOR

Mary Leete has a B.S. degree in Computer Science from Rutgers University and has worked in many areas of professional software engineering. She especially enjoys ActionScript programming. She also has an M.A. in Professional Writing from Maharishi University of Management and has taught courses in writing on the university level.

COLOPHON

This book was produced electronically in Indianapolis, Indiana. Microsoft Word 97 was used for word processing; design and layout were produced using QuarkXPress 4.11 and Adobe Photoshop 5.5 on Power Macintosh computers. The typeface families used are Chicago Laser, Minion, Myriad, Myriad Multiple Master, Prestige Elite, Symbol, Trajan, and Zapf Dingbats.

Acquisitions Editor: **Tom Heine**
Project Editor: **Amanda Peterson**
Technical Editor: **Kyle Bowen**
Copy Editor: **Beth Taylor**
Permissions Editor: **Laura Moss**
Production Coordinator: **Dale White**
Cover Art: **Dale Divoky, Gurdy Leete, Mary Leete, Radim Schreiber**
Quality Control Technicians: **Andy Hollandbeck, Linda Quiqley, Charles Spencer**
Production: **LeAndra Johnson, Laurie Petrone**
Proofreading: **Vicki Broyles**
Indexing: **Johnna VanHoose**

INDEX

A

ActionScript
  buttons, input text, 60–61
  calculator, 204–206
  cascading menus, 160–161, 162–164
  clock, analog/digital, 183–184
  collapsible menu, 144–146
  custom cursors, 158
  drum set, 197
  dynamic scrolling text box, 125–126
  fireworks and, 41, 42–45
  interactive shadows, 110
  magnifying lens, 88–89
  masks, xscale, 37
  mouse trails, 116–117
  MP3 player, 191–194
  multiple choice quiz, 133–134
  music keyboard, 186–187
  news ticker, 178–179
  on/off sound button, 81–82
  paint program, 200–201
  preloader display bar, 168–169
  rollover scrolling, 154–155
  user response form, 136–137
  validation form, 140–142
  volume control slider, 81–82
  zooming/panning, 100–102
AIFF files, 11
analog clock, 181–184
animation. *See also* cartooning
  arm movement, 9
  bubbles, 26–27
    rising bubbles, 28
  buttons, 165–166
  cursors, 157–158
  dragging, 91–93
  drawing and, 3–4
  forward motion, 9
  frame-by-frame, 7
  movie clip conversion, panoramas
      and, 104–105
  positions, creating, 8–9

  preloader bar, 168
  reversing, 4
  text
    growing letters, 65–66
    inside text, 69–70
    keyframes, 65
    layers, 64, 66
    shape tweens, 64
    warping, 63–66
  3D book as user interface, 151
applications on CD-ROM, 210–211
arm movement, walking characters, 9
arrow buttons, rollover scrolling, 153–154
astronaut file, 8

B

backgrounds
  dynamic scrolling text box, 125
  masks, draggable, 107
  mouse trails, 116
  rollover scrolling, 154
  validation form, 142
bar, tabbed menu, 120
base drum, drum set, 196–197
beams, fireworks, 41–42
bitmaps
  fades, 20
  vectors and, 19–20
bubbles
  animation, 26–27
    rising bubbles, 28
  color, 26
  creating, 25–26
  fills, 26
  opaqueness, 26
  popping, sound, 25–28
  sounds, 25
  transparency, 26

buttons
  animated, 165–166
  arrow buttons, rollover scrolling, 153–154
  cascading menus, 159–160, 160–161
  collapsible menus, 143–144
  input text and, 60
  masks, draggable, 108
  in movie clips, 92
  MP3 player, 190
  multiple choice quiz buttons, 131–132
  on/off sound, 79–82
  paint program, 199–200
  pop-up window display, 128–129
  pushbuttons, validation form, 140
  scrollers and, 96
  slider bar, 80–82
  user response form, 136
  zooming/panning and, 100
    ActionScript, 102

C

calculator, 203–206
cartooning, 7–9. *See also* animation
  tweening and, 7
cascading menus, 159–164
CD-ROM accompanying book, 209–211
centering, images, 99
centering text, 63–64
characters
  animating, 7–8
  fills, 9
  walking, 7–9
circles, drawing, strokes, 26
clock, digital/analog, 181–184
collapsible menus, 143–147
color, bubbles, 26
ComboBoxes, scroll bars, 123–124
complex images, drawing, 3–4
compression, video, 84
control, text controlling objects, 59–61

conversions
  photographs to vectors, 19–20
  tweens to symbols, 36
counter, MP3 player, 190
cover-up shapes, 4–5
cursor, draggable, interactive shadows, 110
cursors, custom, 157–158
cymbal, drum set, 196–197

D

digital clock, 181–184
DirectX, video, importing, 83–84
draggable items
  cursor, interactive shadows, 110
  magnifying lens, 87–89
  masks, 107–108
  movies, 91–93, 108
drawing
  animation and, 3–4
  circles, strokes and, 26
  complex images, 3–4
  magnifying glass, 87–88
  talking head, 12–13
drum set, 195–197
dynamic text
  scrolling text box, 124
  validation form, 140

E

earth, rotating, 53–55
ebook version of *50 Fast Flash MX
    Techniques*, 211
effects, slide show transitions, 173
Eraser tool, 4
erasing, images, 4

F

fades
  bitmaps, 20
  outlines, 22
  photographs, morphing and, 23
  vectors, 20
files, sound, importing, 11–12

fills
  bubbles, 26
  characters, 9
filmstrip
  rollover scrolling, 154
  scrolling and, 95–97
fireworks, 41–45
  ActionScript and, 42–45
  beams, 41–42
  positioning, 45
Flash Movies, frame rate,
    synchronization, 84
Flash MX, sound editing, 12
flipping, 38–39
flying letters, 63–65
fonts, MyPager, 71–72
forms, validation, 139–142
forward motion, 9
frame-by-frame animation, 7. *See also*
    cartooning
frame rate, video synchronization, 84
frames
  collapsible menus, 144
  user response form, 136
Free Transform tool, 4

G

glowing text, 76
grooves, 35
growing letters, 65–66

I

images
  centering, 99
  drawing, complex, 3–4
  erasing, 4
  linear, 4–5
  magnifying, 88
  morphing, from shapes, 21–24
  panning, 99–102
  panoramic, 103–105
  simple, 4–5
  slide scroller, motion blur and, 95–97
  zooming, 99–102
importing
  photographs, 15–16
  sound files, 11–12, 80–82
  video, 83–84

input text, 59
  buttons and, 60
  text boxes, 60
installation, CD-ROM
  Macintosh, 210
  Windows, 209–210
instances
  alignment, 37
  text controlling objects, 59–60
interactive shadows, 109–111

K

kaleidoscope, 31–33
  tweens, 32–33
keyboard, 185–187
keyframes
  animated text, 65
  fireworks beams, 42
  intervals, video, 84
  selecting multiple, 4
  sound, 12

L

labels, tabbed menu, 121
layers
  animated text, 64, 66
  multiple choice quiz, 131
  slide show transitions, 172
  tabbed menus, 119–121
letters, flying, 63–65
levitation, walking characters, 9
Library, sound, 12
linear images, 4–5
logo, 3D, rotating, 49–51

M

Macintosh, CD software installation, 210
Macintosh system requirements, CD-ROM
    with book, 209
magnifying glass
  drawing, 87–88
  image import, 88
magnifying lens, draggable, 87–89
maps, rotating earth and, 53–54

masks
  animation inside text, 70
  bubble animation and, 29
  draggable, 107–108
  kaleidoscope, 33
  panoramas, 105
  rollover scrolling, 154
  warping and, 36
  warping images, mask xscale, 37
  zooming and, 100
menus
  cascading, 159–164
  collapsible menus, 143–147
  tabbed menu, 119–121
morphing
  outlines, 22
  shapes, into images, 21–24
  text, 67–68
  tweening, 22–23
  to vector image, 24
motion blur
  layer, adding, 97
  scrolling and, 95–97
motion tweens
  flipping and, 38–39
  kaleidoscope, 32–33
  panoramas, 104
  rotating earth, 54–55
  swarming dots, 72
mouse trails, 115–117
mouth shapes, talking heads and, 13
Movie Explorer, troubleshooting and, 39
movies
  buttons in clips, 92
  creating, 93
  draggable, 91–93, 108
  Magnifier button, 88
  masks, draggable, 107–108
  resizing clips, 92
  stand-alone, 207–208
  as symbols, 91–92
moving bar symbol, warping and, 36
MP3 files, 11
MP3 player, 189–193
multiple choice quiz, 131–134
music keyboard, 185–187
MyPager font, 71–72

N
news ticker, 177–179

O
on/off sound button creation, 79–82
on-screen paint program, 199–201
onion-skinning, 9
opaqueness, bubbles, 26
outlines
  fades, 22
  morphing and, 22
ovals, ripples and, 16

P
paint program, 199–201
panning images, 99–102
panoramic images, 103–105
photographs
  converting to vector, 19–20
  fades, morphing and, 23
  importing, 15–16, 19–20
  morphing to, 21
  stage, 20
  symbols, changing to, 16
piano keyboard, 185–187
popping bubbles, 27
pop-up windows, 127–129
positioning
  animation and, 8–9
  fireworks, 45
preloader, progress display, 167–169
progress bar display, 167–169
Property inspector, sound, 12
pushbuttons, validation form, 140

Q
questions, multiple choice quiz, 132
QuickTime, video, importing, 83–84

R
radiating text effects, 75–76
radio buttons, multiple choice quiz
    buttons, 131–132
rectangles, preloader bar, 167–168
reversing animation, 4
ripples, 15
  creating, 16
  shaping in, 16
  tweening and, 17

rising bubbles animation, 28
rollover scrolling, 153–155
rotating
  earth, 53–55
  fireworks beams, 42
  3D logo, 49–51

S
scoring, multiple choice quiz, 132–133
scroll bars, 123–126
scrolling
  buttons and, 96
  motion blur and, 95–97
  rollover scrolling, 153–155
  virtual reality panorama, 103–105
shadows, interactive, 109–111
shape tweens, 5
  animated text, 66
  radiating text effects, 76
  text animation, 64
  text morphing, 68
shapes
  cover-up shapes, 4–5
  morphing, into images, 21–24
  wedge, kaleidoscope, 31–32
SimpleSound, 11
slide scrollers, images, 95–97
slide shows, transitions, special
    effects, 171–173
sliders, volume control, 79–82
snare drum, drum set, 196
software, CD-ROM, installation
  Macintosh, 210
  Windows, 209–210
sound files
  bubbles, 25
  drum set, 197
  Flash MX, 12
  importing, 11–12, 80–82
  Library, 12
  music keyboard, 186
Sound Recorder, 11
special effects, slide show transitions,
    171–173
stage, photographs, 20
stand-alone movie, 207–208
static text, 59
stop actions, 20
  3D book as user interface, 152
strokes, circles, drawing, 26

submenus, collapsible menu, 146
swarming dots, text and, 71–73
symbols
  changing photographs to, 16
  converting tweens to, 36
  dots, swarming to form text, 72
  movies as, 91–92
  ripples and, 16
  text controlling objects, 59–61
synthesizer, 185–187
system requirements, CD-ROM with
    book, 209

T
tabbed menu, 119–121
tabs, tabbed menu, 120
talking heads, 11–13
  sound files, importing, 11–12
text
  animation
    growing letters, 65–66
    inside text, 69–70
    keyframes, 65
    layers, 64, 66
    shape tweens, 64
    warping, 63–66
  centering, 63–64
  glowing, 76
  input text, 59
  morphing, 67–68
  news ticker, 177–178
  radiating effects, 75–76
  shadows, interactive, 109–111
  static, 59
  swarming dots, 71–73
text boxes
  calculator, 204
  dynamic scrolling text box, 124
  input text, 60
  news ticker, 179
  user response form, 135–136
  validation form, 139–140

text controlling objects, 59–61
text, softening edges, 76
3D book as user interface, 149–152
3D logo, rotating, 49–51
Timeline
  cascading menus, 161
  draggable movie, 93
  menus, collapsible, 146–147
  walking characters and, 8
tools
  Eraser, 4
  Free Transform, 4
transitions, slide shows, special effects,
    171–173
transparency, bubbles, 26
troubleshooting CD-ROM, 211
tweening
  cartooning and, 7
  morphing and, 22–23
  motion tweens, kaleidoscope, 32–33
  ripples and, 17
  shape tweens, 5

U
user interface, 3D book as, 149–152
user response form, 135–137

V
validation form, 139–142
variables, text boxes, 60
vectors
  bitmaps, 19–20
  fades, 20
  morphing to, 24
  photographs, converting, 19–20
video
  compression, 84
  frame ratio, 84
  importing, 83–84

keyframe intervals, 84
  settings, 84
virtual reality panorama, 103–105
volume control, slider, 79–82

W
walking astronaut file, 8
walking characters, 7–9
  arm movement, 9
  forward motion, 9
  levitation, 9
  positions, creating, 8–9
  Timeline and, 8
warping images, 35–39
  flipping, 38–39
  wave and, 35–36
warping text, 63–66
WAV files, 11
waves, warping and, 35–37
wedge shapes, kaleidoscope and, 31–32
Windows, CD software installation, 209–210
windows, pop-up windows, 127–129
Windows system requirements, CD-ROM
    with book, 209

X
xscale, 37

Y
yscale, 37

Z
zooming images, 99–102

WILEY PUBLISHING
END-USER LICENSE AGREEMENT

PREAMBLE

The licenses for most software are designed to take away your freedom to share and change it. By contrast, the GNU General Public License is intended to guarantee your freedom to share and change free software — to make sure the software is free for all its users. This General Public License applies to most of the Free Software Foundation's software and to any other program whose authors commit to using it. (Some other Free Software Foundation software is covered by the GNU Library General Public License instead.) You can apply it to your programs, too.

When we speak of free software, we are referring to freedom, not price. Our General Public Licenses are designed to make sure that you have the freedom to distribute copies of free software (and charge for this service if you wish), that you receive source code or can get it if you want it, that you can change the software or use pieces of it in new free programs; and that you know you can do these things.

To protect your rights, we need to make restrictions that forbid anyone to deny you these rights or to ask you to surrender the rights. These restrictions translate to certain responsibilities for you if you distribute copies of the software, or if you modify it.

For example, if you distribute copies of such a program, whether gratis or for a fee, you must give the recipients all the rights that you have. You must make sure that they, too, receive or can get the source code. And you must show them these terms so they know their rights.

We protect your rights with two steps: (1) copyright the software, and (2) offer you this license which gives you legal permission to copy, distribute and/or modify the software.

Also, for each author's protection and ours, we want to make certain that everyone understands that there is no warranty for this free software. If the software is modified by someone else and passed on, we want its recipients to know that what they have is not the original, so that any problems introduced by others will not reflect on the original authors' reputations.

Finally, any free program is threatened constantly by software patents. We wish to avoid the danger that redistributors of a free program will individually obtain patent licenses, in effect making the program proprietary. To prevent this, we have made it clear that any patent must be licensed for everyone's free use or not licensed at all.

The precise terms and conditions for copying, distribution and modification follow.

TERMS AND CONDITIONS FOR COPYING, DISTRIBUTION, AND MODIFICATION

0. This License applies to any program or other work which contains a notice placed by the copyright holder saying it may be distributed under the terms of this General Public License. The "Program", below, refers to any such program or work, and a "work based on the Program" means either the Program or any derivative work under copyright law: that is to say, a work containing the Program or a portion of it, either verbatim or with modifications and/or translated into another language. (Hereinafter, translation is included without limitation in the term "modification.") Each licensee is addressed as "you."

223

Activities other than copying, distribution and modification are not covered by this License; they are outside its scope. The act of running the Program is not restricted, and the output from the Program is covered only if its contents constitute a work based on the Program (independent of having been made by running the Program). Whether that is true depends on what the Program does.

1. You may copy and distribute verbatim copies of the Program's source code as you receive it, in any medium, provided that you conspicuously and appropriately publish on each copy an appropriate copyright notice and disclaimer of warranty; keep intact all the notices that refer to this License and to the absence of any warranty; and give any other recipients of the Program a copy of this License along with the Program.

You may charge a fee for the physical act of transferring a copy, and you may at your option offer warranty protection in exchange for a fee.

2. You may modify your copy or copies of the Program or any portion of it, thus forming a work based on the Program, and copy and distribute such modifications or work under the terms of Section 1 above, provided that you also meet all of these conditions:

    (a) You must cause the modified files to carry prominent notices stating that you changed the files and the date of any change.

    (b) You must cause any work that you distribute or publish, that in whole or in part contains or is derived from the Program or any part thereof, to be licensed as a whole at no charge to all third parties under the terms of this License.

    (c) If the modified program normally reads commands interactively when run, you must cause it, when started running for such interactive use in the most ordinary way, to print or display an announcement including an appropriate copyright notice and a notice that there is no warranty (or else, saying that you provide a warranty) and that users may redistribute the program under these conditions, and telling the user how to view a copy of this License. (Exception: if the Program itself is interactive but does not normally print such an announcement, your work based on the Program is not required to print an announcement.)

    These requirements apply to the modified work as a whole. If identifiable sections of that work are not derived from the Program, and can be reasonably considered independent and separate works in themselves, then this License, and its terms, do not apply to those sections when you distribute them as separate works. But when you distribute the same sections as part of a whole which is a work based on the Program, the distribution of the whole must be on the terms of this License, whose permissions for other licensees extend to the entire whole, and thus to each and every part regardless of who wrote it.

    Thus, it is not the intent of this section to claim rights or contest your rights to work written entirely by you; rather, the intent is to exercise the right to control the distribution of derivative or collective works based on the Program.

    In addition, mere aggregation of another work not based on the Program with the Program (or with a work based on the Program) on a volume of a storage or distribution medium does not bring the other work under the scope of this License.

3. You may copy and distribute the Program (or a work based on it, under Section 2) in object code or executable form under the terms of Sections 1 and 2 above provided that you also do one of the following:

(a) Accompany it with the complete corresponding machine-readable source code, which must be distributed under the terms of Sections 1 and 2 above on a medium customarily used for software interchange; or,

(b) Accompany it with a written offer, valid for at least three years, to give any third party, for a charge no more than your cost of physically performing source distribution, a complete machine-readable copy of the corresponding source code, to be distributed under the terms of Sections 1 and 2 above on a medium customarily used for software interchange; or,

(c) Accompany it with the information you received as to the offer to distribute corresponding source code. (This alternative is allowed only for noncommercial distribution and only if you received the program in object code or executable form with such an offer, in accord with Subsection b above.)

The source code for a work means the preferred form of the work for making modifications to it. For an executable work, complete source code means all the source code for all modules it contains, plus any associated interface definition files, plus the scripts used to control compilation and installation of the executable. However, as a special exception, the source code distributed need not include anything that is normally distributed (in either source or binary form) with the major components (compiler, kernel, and so on) of the operating system on which the executable runs, unless that component itself accompanies the executable.

If distribution of executable or object code is made by offering access to copy from a designated place, then offering equivalent access to copy the source code from the same place counts as distribution of the source code, even though third parties are not compelled to copy the source along with the object code.

4. You may not copy, modify, sublicense, or distribute the Program except as expressly provided under this License. Any attempt otherwise to copy, modify, sublicense or distribute the Program is void, and will automatically terminate your rights under this License. However, parties who have received copies, or rights, from you under this License will not have their licenses terminated so long as such parties remain in full compliance.

5. You are not required to accept this License, since you have not signed it. However, nothing else grants you permission to modify or distribute the Program or its derivative works. These actions are prohibited by law if you do not accept this License. Therefore, by modifying or distributing the Program (or any work based on the Program), you indicate your acceptance of this License to do so, and all its terms and conditions for copying, distributing or modifying the Program or works based on it.

6. Each time you redistribute the Program (or any work based on the Program), the recipient automatically receives a license from the original licensor to copy, distribute or modify the Program subject to these terms and conditions. You may not impose any further restrictions on the recipients' exercise of the rights granted herein. You are not responsible for enforcing compliance by third parties to this License.

7 If, as a consequence of a court judgment or allegation of patent infringement or for any other reason (not limited to patent issues), conditions are imposed on you (whether by court order, agreement or otherwise) that contradict the conditions of this License, they do not excuse you from the conditions of this License. If you cannot distribute so as to satisfy simultaneously your obligations under this License and any other pertinent obligations, then as a consequence you may not distribute the Program at all. For example, if a patent license would not permit royalty-free redistribution of the Program by all those who receive copies directly or indirectly through you, then the only way you could satisfy both it and this License would be to refrain entirely from distribution of the Program.

If any portion of this section is held invalid or unenforceable under any particular circumstance, the balance of the section is intended to apply and the section as a whole is intended to apply in other circumstances.

It is not the purpose of this section to induce you to infringe any patents or other property right claims or to contest validity of any such claims; this section has the sole purpose of protecting the integrity of the free software distribution system, which is implemented by public license practices. Many people have made generous contributions to the wide range of software distributed through that system in reliance on consistent application of that system; it is up to the author/donor to decide if he or she is willing to distribute software through any other system and a licensee cannot impose that choice.

This section is intended to make thoroughly clear what is believed to be a consequence of the rest of this License.

8. If the distribution and/or use of the Program is restricted in certain countries either by patents or by copyrighted interfaces, the original copyright holder who places the Program under this License may add an explicit geographical distribution limitation excluding those countries, so that distribution is permitted only in or among countries not thus excluded. In such case, this License incorporates the limitation as if written in the body of this License.

9. The Free Software Foundation may publish revised and/or new versions of the General Public License from time to time. Such new versions will be similar in spirit to the present version, but may differ in detail to address new problems or concerns.

Each version is given a distinguishing version number. If the Program specifies a version number of this License which applies to it and "any later version", you have the option of following the terms and conditions either of that version or of any later version published by the Free Software Foundation. If the Program does not specify a version number of this License, you may choose any version ever published by the Free Software Foundation.

10. If you wish to incorporate parts of the Program into other free programs whose distribution conditions are different, write to the author to ask for permission. For software which is copyrighted by the Free Software Foundation, write to the Free Software Foundation; we sometimes make exceptions for this. Our decision will be guided by the two goals of preserving the free status of all derivatives of our free software and of promoting the sharing and reuse of software generally.

NO WARRANTY

11. BECAUSE THE PROGRAM IS LICENSED FREE OF CHARGE, THERE IS NO WARRANTY FOR THE PROGRAM, TO THE EXTENT PERMITTED BY APPLICABLE LAW. EXCEPT WHEN OTHERWISE STATED IN WRITING THE COPYRIGHT HOLDERS AND/OR OTHER PARTIES PROVIDE THE PROGRAM "AS IS" WITHOUT WARRANTY OF ANY KIND, EITHER EXPRESSED OR IMPLIED, INCLUDING, BUT NOT LIMITED TO, THE IMPLIED WARRANTIES OF MERCHANTABILITY AND FITNESS FOR A PARTICULAR PURPOSE. THE ENTIRE RISK AS TO THE QUALITY AND PERFORMANCE OF THE PROGRAM IS WITH YOU. SHOULD THE PROGRAM PROVE DEFECTIVE, YOU ASSUME THE COST OF ALL NECESSARY SERVICING, REPAIR, OR CORRECTION.

12. IN NO EVENT UNLESS REQUIRED BY APPLICABLE LAW OR AGREED TO IN WRITING WILL ANY COPYRIGHT HOLDER, OR ANY OTHER PARTY WHO MAY MODIFY AND/OR REDISTRIBUTE THE PROGRAM AS PERMITTED ABOVE, BE LIABLE TO YOU FOR DAMAGES, INCLUDING ANY GENERAL, SPECIAL, INCIDENTAL OR CONSEQUENTIAL DAMAGES ARISING OUT OF THE USE OR INABILITY TO USE THE PROGRAM (INCLUDING BUT NOT LIMITED TO LOSS OF DATA OR DATA BEING RENDERED INACCURATE OR LOSSES SUSTAINED BY YOU OR THIRD PARTIES OR A FAILURE OF THE PROGRAM TO OPERATE WITH ANY OTHER PROGRAMS), EVEN IF SUCH HOLDER OR OTHER PARTY HAS BEEN ADVISED OF THE POSSIBILITY OF SUCH DAMAGES.

END OF TERMS AND CONDITIONS